"Love+Joy+Peace+Patience+Goodness+Kindness+Gentleness +Faithfulness+Self Control—9 attributes which, in my opinion, describe my friend Sonny Sandoval's character precisely. I'm confident that you will agree as you dive into his amazing new book, *Son of Southtown: My Life Between Two Worlds*. Sonny would shy away from this statement and say he's not perfect. Obviously true. All of us are beautifully flawed. But Sonny comfortably displays these 9 characteristics more genuinely than most I've met in my life. In *Son of Southtown* you will find that Sonny is always shining in the crazy entertainment business he and I live in, and he shines just as bright in his personal life when the crowds aren't there to see. A hero of the faith to me since 2005, Sonny Sandoval has been an encouragement to me since day one, and I will love+support this Son of Southtown and everything he does forever."

Brian "Head" Welch, cofounder of the Grammy Award–winning band Korn; *New York Times* bestselling author of *Save Me from Myself*, *Stronger*, and *With My Eyes Wide Open*; and costar of the Showtime documentary *Loud Krazy Love*

"I've always had mad respect for Sonny. From watching him in the early years and throughout his career, he has always lived his life and pursued his music with sincere authenticity. And he has remained true to the faith that runs deep within him."

TobyMac, Grammy-winning artist

"Sonny is the most genuine, loving, and loyal person I've ever had the privilege of knowing. In him, I see the very characteristics of Christ lived out in day-to-day life. His wisdom and example have had a profound and lasting impact on my own life. Sonny's authenticity and Christ-like nature are recognized not just by his family and friends but by all who have the opportunity to know him—from renowned musicians and athletes to respected pastors. He is truly the "real deal," and his life and character have the power to inspire and uplift all who encounter him."

Ryan Ries, cofounder of The Whosoevers, author, and radio host of *The Ryan Ries Show*

"This book is such an open, honest look into Sonny Sandoval's life. His story, his music, and his walk with Christ continues to inspire me and many others."

Jacoby Shaddix, frontman for Papa Roach

"Sonny has had a profound and prolific impact globally in both the secular and Christian world. His musical talent and creative ability stand up to some of the greatest musicians of his time. His dedication to giving God all the glory has been an inspiration not only to myself but to an entire generation."

Paul Teutul Jr., founder of Paul Jr. Designs

"Having faced the demands of a high-profile career, I can attest to the authenticity of Sonny's story. His book goes beyond rock and roll, offering a profound account of his personal growth and unwavering faith in God. Sonny's steadfast belief has guided him through challenges and shaped his journey, highlighting the significance of his relationships with both his family and his band."

Rey 619 Mysterio, professional wrestler

"Sonny's journey is nothing short of inspiring. *Son of Southtown* is a powerful testament to the resilience of the human spirit, guided by faith. Sonny's story of overcoming adversity, finding true faith, and rising to the top of the music world is a must-read for anyone seeking hope and purpose."

Andy Vargas, lead vocalist for Carlos Santana

"Sonny's journey hasn't been easy. But the pain and struggle he's been through has only made his faith and PMA (positive mental attitude) stronger. And as someone who lost a parent as well, I can relate. Also there are only a few musicians that really live their lyrics off stage, and Sonny is one of them. He's very inspiring to me and millions of people around the world. Honored to call him my friend."

Toby Morse, H2O singer and host of *One Life One Chance* podcast

SON OF SOUTHTOWN

MY LIFE BETWEEN TWO WORLDS

SONNY SANDOVAL

BakerBooks

a division of Baker Publishing Group
Grand Rapids, Michigan

Published by Baker Books
a division of Baker Publishing Group
Grand Rapids, Michigan
BakerBooks.com

Printed in the United States of America

Library of Congress Cataloging-in-Publication Data
Names: Sandoval, Sonny, 1974– author.
Title: Son of Southtown : my life between two worlds / Sonny Sandoval.
Description: Grand Rapids : Baker Books, a division of Baker Publishing
    Group, 2025. | Includes bibliographical references.
Identifiers: LCCN 2024023220 | ISBN 9781540904423 (cloth) | ISBN
    9781493447060 (ebook)
Subjects: LCSH: Sandoval, Sonny, 1974– | Rap musicians—California—
    San Diego—Biography. | Singers—California—San Diego—Biography. |
    Sandoval, Sonny, 1974—Religion.
Classification: LCC ML420.S1425 A3 2025 | DDC 782.421649092 [B]—dc23/
    eng/20240521
LC record available at https://lccn.loc.gov/2024023220

Scripture quotations are from the King James Version of the Bible.

Cover design by Faceout Studio, Molly von Borstel

The "I AM" lyrics are © Capitol CMG Publishing, Concord Music Publishing LLC, Kobalt Music Publishing Ltd.

The "Alive" lyrics are © Sony/atv Harmony, Souljah Music, Firematic Music.

Published in association with Yates & Yates, www.yates2.com.

Baker Publishing Group publications use paper produced from sustainable forestry practices and postconsumer waste whenever possible.

25 26 27 28 29 30 31   7 6 5 4 3 2 1

To my mother, who shared her Jesus with me.

And to my Noni, who gave her family everything
and asked for nothing in return.
You were truly an angel walking this earth.

CONTENTS

FOREWORD

The first time I saw P.O.D. play live was the very same day that my friends and I decided to name our band Switchfoot. We were an opening band sharing the bill with P.O.D.—a band that we had always heard about but had never seen live. When they came onstage, the whole room was transformed. Everything changed. I was blown away by the intensity and the authenticity in the music. The strength. The personality.

And from that point on, Sonny Sandoval has been an inspiration for me both on and offstage. In an industry of facades and frauds, he has been an example of how to be real. How to be true. Kind, yet strong. Unafraid to be genuinely himself.

In some ways, our stories are very similar. We both grew up surfing, skating, and playing music in San Diego. Yet, in other ways, we're worlds apart: Sonny and his crew are from Southtown. My bandmates and I are from North County. Two very different sides of the same city. And yet, he's always treated us like family. I think of Sonny as the older, stronger, wiser cousin that's always been there when I needed anything.

I'm always thankful for every conversation we've shared, and yet I've never truly known the intricacies of his past. This book reveals the complexity of that story, the sparks that forged the fire behind his eyes. This book tells his story with authenticity, candor, and humor.

Ralph Waldo Emerson says, "To be yourself in a world that is constantly trying to make you something else is the greatest accomplishment." This book is the tale of someone who has endeavored to do just that.

Jon Foreman
lead singer of Switchfoot
San Diego, California

1

MAITLAND AVENUE

Two sides.

To the left is rock and roll. Fame and fortune. World travel, wining, dining. All that hype about sex, drugs, and rock and roll? Dude, let me tell you, it's a real thing. Total freedom to do whatever you want to do, whenever you want to do it, and with whomever happens to be available at the time.

To the right is the church. Sure, it's got its own promises of happiness, peace, and salvation. But with traditional Christianity comes rules, and let's face it, rules kinda suck. You've got to look like me, talk like me, and learn all-new definitions for the word *fun*. Some say, "But would you really choose a temporary high over eternal life?" The answer may seem obvious, but it isn't. Eternal life is a promise you've got to wait on for some time in the future. In the here and now, though, there are some pretty good highs around, and you don't have to look too far to find them.

Welcome to my world. I've been walking this line between the secular and the sacred for three decades, and I'm still on that same road today. Each side is pulling me their way, and there are a lot of people who get pissed off when I refuse to follow them. Listen, I know I've got a reputation. Sonny Sandoval, lead singer of P.O.D. He's the Christian dude with the dreads in that nu metal band. If that's what you know of me, then congrats, you nailed it. That's all true.

But condensing my life to a couple simple sentences is like saying, "Yeah, I know all about electricity. I flip the switch, and boom, there's light." We've all got our stories. No one's is any better than anyone else's. It's just that some journeys take roads that are a little less traveled. Mine happens to include a childhood growing up in the hood, building a band up from scratch, hitting it big and selling millions of albums, then watching that band fall apart and come back together—more than once. And don't forget that balance of trying to stay true to my God while hanging out in the devil's playground.

Wouldn't it be easier to choose one side or the other? Undoubtedly. But I can't. I'm on a mission, and that mission is the primary purpose of my life. That is what keeps me on the razor's edge. Now, I could come right out and tell you what that mission is, but what fun would that be? Besides, I'm no teacher, and I'm certainly not a preacher. I'm a musician, which means I'm a storyteller, and this is my story. And because all great stories must have a great beginning, here's mine:

Once upon a time in Southtown . . .

THERE IS A DIRTY BEAUTY to my city. San Diego, California, is a Top 10 tourist destination and deservedly so. But hidden beneath the eye-catching veneer of Coronado Island and Old Town and Balboa Park is the real world that I grew up in. You won't find my Southtown on a postcard. It isn't gracing the cover of any vacation brochure. From the house I grew up in, it will take half the drive to get you to downtown Tijuana than it would to get you into the heart of San Diego. My city is one of drug traffickers and border crossers. It's one of poverty and petty crime.

Don't get me wrong. I love this city. You open my veins, and I bleed San Diego brown. I didn't choose to be born here, but I chose to stay to this day. This city is part of me. God created me, but it was Southtown that made me.

THE BORDERS OF SOUTHTOWN are the subject of many backyard barbecue debates. The clinical, upper-middle-class definition says that if you're driving down from LA, once you cross the 8 freeway, you're in Southtown. But not my people. The hardcore say you've got to keep cruising the 5 to get to the real Southtown. The more hardcore they are, the farther south you've got to go.

My Southtown is past the signs for National City and Chula Vista. It's on the other side of the pitiful Otay River. When my Southtown looks west, it doesn't find the scenic lighthouse of Point Loma. It sees the eighteen-foot border fence of Imperial Beach. This is where you'll find the true Southtown. If you're looking for the corner of the United States, my hood is as bottom left as you can get.

Life at two exits from the border comes with some givens. There has always been a flood of crossings—legal and illegal. Drugs have always moved through the area, and cartel business is constantly spilling over from Mexico. It was impossible to grow up in my neighborhood and not know that craziness was there. A lot of my friends had dealings with guys from down south. People I know have been kidnapped and held for ransom. Others got caught up in the drugs and the dealing, then just disappeared.

Looking back now, it's easy to make judgments. "What were those kids doing messing around in all that drug business? Didn't they know how dangerous it was?" But that's old dude thinking. That's people from the outside looking in. When you're a kid, you just don't see it like that. Would you rather go work construction for ten hours a day or do a little selling and make five times as much? Besides, when you're young, you feel invincible. It's those other guys that get hit, not me.

My early years were the time of eighties gangster rap. Everybody wanted to be gangsta-hard. Everybody wanted to be a thug. That was just the mentality of the time. The only thing that kept me from following the same paths was this inner conviction that I wanted to do something different with my life than end up warehoused in a prison or buried somewhere down in Baja.

I watched some of my homies take the wrong path. Crossing the border was so much easier back then, and some of my boys had families on the other side. Without a second thought, we could stuff everyone in a few cars, drive across the border, hit our favorite taco stand for dinner, and still make it back home in time to kick back with the homies who weren't able to roll with us this time. If you were ever willing to take the risk of hiding away a little something something to bring back to the States, then you did just that.

Unfortunately, often after a few successful "little something something" trips came the temptation to try to bump it up to a bigger something something. I watched some of my crew go that route. Weed was like the entry level, and it went down from there. How deep you went was up to you. Before you knew it, you could easily find yourself a lot farther on the other side of the law than you originally expected. I'd give you details about a couple of my homies, but quite honestly, I'm already a little nervous about saying what I've said so far.

For my inner group, though, there was an innocence about it all. They weren't the ones watching the gangster movies and wanting to go all Pacino on people. It was just how life played out down in Southtown. We'd watch older friends who were suddenly rolling up in a Mercedes. It was hard not to be like, "Dude, that's how you do it. That's who I want to be." It totally had to be divine intervention that I was never impressed with that kind of stuff. In the mathematics of way too many Southtown teen guys, if "a + b = Mercedes" then sign me up!

Sadly, I saw a lot of the guys who followed that equation go to prison. In fact, most of my best friends have done time at one point or another. Some of them are still there. Others got out and tried to live the straight life, but it's not easy once you've been inside. Life is stacked against you. One of our homies' older brothers went in and out a bunch. The last time he was released, he ended up getting hooked on his own product. One night he drove down the freeway the wrong way and killed a family. Now he's paralyzed and doing life. Imagine life in prison. Now imagine it in a wheelchair. To this day when I think about it, it breaks my heart—both for my buddy and especially for the people who lost their lives.

Around that same time, one of my crew was at a house party. He was in the kitchen, and this guy jumped him. My friend was getting pounded, so he reached for something to defend himself with. His hand closed on a kitchen knife, and he plunged it into the dude and killed him. We tried to get him to stay and plead self-defense, but he freaked out and fled to Mexico. Hiding out south of the border rarely leads to good clean living. My buddy just got deeper into stuff, until he finally crossed back over. When he did, he was arrested and ended up doing twenty-two years. He found the Lord in prison and got his life cleaned up. Now he's out and realizing that this city isn't kind to ex-cons. That's especially true of Christian ex-cons who are trying to keep themselves on the straight. Still, he's doing his best to stay out of trouble and is helping others to not make the same mistakes he made. Around here, that's called a success story.

Before you start making any "You do the crime, you do the time" judgments, realize that this was just the Southtown culture. Drugs were everywhere. There was a time when I was living with a bunch of my friends, and they all got big into these downers. Everyone was dropping these pills all the time. I was working night shift, so I missed a lot of the partying. I came home one morning, and they were just rolling in. They were going on about the awesome time they had at this party. But when they woke up the next day, they couldn't even remember getting back to the house.

I love those guys. They were my crew. But there was something in me that kept me from falling into those traps. It was a conviction, a resolve that I wasn't going to become another San Diego statistic. But the origin story of that innate ability to say "no" doesn't begin in my community of Otay Mesa West but in a poor village on the west coast of Italy.

IF THE BOOT OF ITALY was a Doc Marten, about halfway up the laces you'd find the city of Sorrento. A two-hour hike northeast from that coastal town would bring you to the tiny village of Ticciano. It was in this poverty-stricken hamlet that my grandmother was born. World War II had devastated rural Italy, and the region would struggle for the next few decades. Food was hard to come by. Clothing was shared between siblings. Educational opportunities for young women in the area were nonexistent, and decent jobs were almost as rare. Often, Noni, as we call her, would spend her days working for the rich people outside of her community in exchange for eggs. When she reached her teens, she met a much-older American serviceman stationed nearby, my Grandpa Charles, and the two married. Soon, my mother, Aurelia, was born, and two years later came my Auntie Agnes.

Once, I asked my Noni why her mom would allow her teenage daughter to marry this old guy. Certainly, there was an element of survival to her decision. If you go to where I grew up near the border, you'll see poverty. But my Noni was facing full-on deprivation. So, survival instincts kick in, and you do what you have to do.

But her getting together with my Grandpa Charles was about more than just maintaining her existence on this earth. It was about hope. She was like any other girl her age with dreams about a new life, a better life, maybe even that great love story. If there was any place that dream could happen, it was in America. So, when my Grandpa Charles was transferred back to the US, my Noni crossed the Atlantic with him and her girls. She can still remember her great immigrant moment when their ship sailed into New York, and she saw the Statue of Liberty standing there welcoming her to this land of opportunity. All she could think of was, *My life is going to change.*

By the time my mom turned three, my Noni and Grandpa Charles had moved the whole family to Monterey, California. They stayed there for a short time before finally settling down on Maitland Avenue in south San Diego. I've heard a lot of stories about how life was inside that house, but out of respect for my grandmother, and even for my grandfather, I'm not going to get into details. Let's just say that it didn't turn out to be the great love story she had dreamed of. Before I was old enough to remember him, Grandpa Charles died, and his death provided her the opportunity to close the book on one chapter in her life and open up another.

My Italian Noni had been learning English and now started a restaurant job. Incredibly loyal, she worked in that same restaurant until she just couldn't work anymore. That was the work ethic that poverty taught her. She was determined to do whatever it took for her to achieve her American dream. That grit and work ethic passed on to her kids, her grandkids, and now her great-grandkids.

A number of years after Grandpa Charles died, my Noni met a man named Thomas. Check this out, just like Charles, Thomas was a Guamanian. What are the odds? It's not like Guam is this huge island out in the Pacific Ocean cranking out eligible bachelors. It's essentially just a beautiful speck on the map that's occasionally used as a speed bump to slow down typhoons. Yet, my Noni managed to find two men from Guam—one whom I never knew and one who was the only grandfather I would ever really know.

Just to give you a quick idea of the character of my Grandpa Tom. He was a veteran who survived a full tour in Vietnam. When he got back, he learned that his younger brother had been drafted. Instead of letting his brother risk going to Vietnam, Grandpa Tom snatched up his ID and went in his place, fighting through a second tour of duty. That's how much he loved his family. It was that kind of love he brought to my Noni. He sacrificed for her, took care of her, and made her feel special. Finally, after all those years, my Noni had her great love story.

To me, my Noni will always be a saint. I'm not saying she was perfect. There were a lot of mistakes along the way, as there are in any family. But more than any other person, she was the center of our Maitland Avenue universe. And she had a lot to do with who I am today.

MY MOM AND MY AUNTIE got pregnant within three months of each other. Mom was eighteen, and Auntie Agnes was two years younger. This happened four months before the *Roe v. Wade* decision in January 1973, and abortion was becoming a much more popular option for young, unwed girls. Thankfully, mom's Catholic roots kept me alive. I was born in May of 1973 at Sharp Memorial Hospital on Clairemont Mesa Boulevard in San Diego. I think it was also some of that Catholic guilt that got my mom and dad to say "I do" to one other.

You'll hear a lot more about Mom in a bit. For now, just know that in my mind, if my Noni was second only to Jesus in saintliness, Mom was pushing a close third. Of course, I didn't recognize this when I was growing up. I was a stubborn, confused kid, and her job was to try to raise me up the right way. It wasn't until later that I realized just how amazing she was.

When I was born, Mom and Dad weren't anywhere near ready to be parents. They were kids having kids. Their marriage was short-lived, and soon they split up. I don't know exactly how old I was when my dad took off. I can't remember him ever being in the home. Mom stepped up and did what it took to raise me as a single mom. Despite her age, she was a rock.

My dad, on the other hand, was a wanderer. I say that with all the mystique and inherent coolness the word implies. Think of Lynyrd Skynyrd's "Free Bird" when the dude finally gives up trying to explain himself to his girl. The lyrics end and the guitars start up and you can picture the guy on his Harley riding off with the wind blowing through his hair. No ties; total freedom. My dad is not the biker type by any means, but he was an absolute free spirit and a free thinker. The only rules that he was going to play by were his own.

Now, in my opinion—and I'm going to say this as kindly as I can—those aren't necessarily the traits that are going to set you up as an ideal husband or father of the year. But there's still something about that mindset that I admire. He did his best to make the situation with my mom and me work, but, as wanderers often do, he'd be here one moment and gone the next. Sucked for me as a young kid, but I get it. If anything, I think it taught me at an early age what kind of husband and father I wanted to be and what kind I was committed not to be.

Dad would usually split his time between Cali and Texas. His mom, my Grandma Hazel, was a beautiful Hawaiian girl, born on the Big Island but adopted and raised on Maui. She too married a serviceman and relocated to the mainland. After leaving paradise, she found herself stranded in Price, Utah. The town was a far stretch from home for this island girl, but she did her best to make a home for my Grandpa Sandy and their four children. I never got the opportunity to really know my Grandpa Sandy other than short visits here and there and maybe a family reunion or two.

I don't know the details on why my grandma and grandpa divorced, but whatever it was, I'm guessing that's why I didn't get the chance to ever get close to him. I do know that I loved him very much, and somehow, some way, even in the short time I got to see him, there was something in his eyes that always assured me that he cared about me and loved me just as much. My short, handsome, Mexican grandfather was a caring, sensitive man. He passed those character traits on to my dad, who passed them on to me.

After their divorce, my Grandma Hazel got remarried to a cowboy out in Odessa, Texas. If you're not sure where Odessa is, just drive to the middle of Texas oil country and hang a left. I got my first name from her new husband, Paul. But, just like everyone calls me Sonny, we all called him Pops. I loved my Pops. He was a good man.

DAD WOULD TYPICALLY head out to Texas and work for six months. Then, suddenly, he'd be back on Maitland Avenue. I'd go crazy every time he showed up. I was just a kid. What did I care about who was to blame for what and how much child support was still owed? I was just excited to have Dad around. I think most kids from broken homes want to believe that Mommy and Daddy will get back together and everyone will live happily ever after. It's not until they're older that they realize it rarely ever happens.

I remember one time when I was with him when I was still a little kid. He decided he wanted to go see Grandpa Sandy, who was now living up in Santa Maria above Santa Barbara. My dad stuck out his thumb, and we hitchhiked up. The couple that picked us up were very nice. They must have seen this little kid crashed out in the back seat of their car with his teddy bear and felt sorry for me. Since we were hitching, they probably figured that Dad didn't have much money. They gave him a few bucks so we could get something to eat.

My dad was from that hitchhiking era. He would still do it today if he needed to. If he spotted a dude on the side of the road, he'd open his door for him. If he needed a ride up the coast, he'd put out his thumb. "You do me a solid, I'll do one for you." That's part of his trusting personality I admire; he always tries to see the good in people. I'm not saying that I go around picking up hitchers. I have a strong aversion to getting axe-murdered. But I often find myself holding out hope for the underdogs even after most others have given up on them.

When I was six, he wanted to visit his friend in Imperial Beach. It was about fifteen minutes away from where I lived, so we hitched our way there. His friend wasn't home, though, so he decided we would wait. I can still feel the heat from the three cement steps that we sat on while we stared at the dead grass in the guy's front yard. While we waited, Dad lit up a joint, took a toke, then passed it to me to see if I would take a hit. I can't even remember if I took a drag. I probably did, just to show my dad I could. To me, it wasn't that big a deal. I had seen family members doing it my whole life.

Today, part of me thinks, *Dude, what were you thinking giving your kid weed?* No doubt, it is 100 percent the wrong thing to do. But I can't help giving my dad somewhat of a pass. I don't think he really saw me as a kid. That's not the way his mind worked. To him, we were buddies, which was true. In fact, we were best buds. What do you do with your best buds? For him, you pass it around. Would I ever do that with my kids? Hell no. And if I'd found out that any adult was giving them some herb when they were still young, we would have had a serious issue. But for some reason, even as an adult, I find myself letting this carefree road warrior father of mine slide on this one.

One more Dad story. Around the same time, he decided that my cousin Wuv and I were going to take a late-night Greyhound with him up to Santa Maria. Definitely an improvement over using the thumb. I have no idea whether he asked permission to take us out of the city. He wasn't the kind of guy who bothered with permissions. He got the urge; we did it. Since it was late, we fell asleep on the bus. He woke us up a little later when the bus pulled up to a convenience store. He said he was going inside and told us to wait for him.

Wuv and I were waiting and waiting, trying not to fall back asleep. Suddenly, the bus doors closed. Then we started rolling. We jumped up and started running down the aisle. "Stop! My dad's in the store! Stop!" The driver pulled the bus over and opened the door. My dad stepped on board, cool as could be. If he hadn't woken us up before he went into the store, who knows how far we would have gotten before someone discovered these two little kids all alone and crashed out in the back.

My relationship with my dad today is okay. When I was a kid, he was everything to me, and we had some great times. But he knew I would soon grow up and find my own best buds, and our time together would get shorter and shorter. These days, my life consists of my wife and my kids. I've got the band and my foundation and a whole bunch of other things going on. I wish there was room in my schedule to make up for lost time, but my life for the last thirty years has been a roller coaster, and I don't know what a daily routine even looks like. I love my dad very much and want nothing but the best for him. I do pray that someday when the dust finally settles, we'll be able to pick up right where we left off so many years ago. Hey, Dad, did I tell you today that I love you?

OVER TIME, MY NONI saved up enough money to buy the house on Maitland Avenue in which she had been living and raising her two daughters. Later, when my mom and Auntie Agnes were old enough to move out, the house next door came up for rent. My Auntie Agnes and Uncle Noah moved in. It was perfect! Even though the two houses weren't attached, they might as well have been. They formed our family living space—the Sandoval compound! At first, Mom and I lived with Grandpa Tom and my Noni, but there were times the pieces shifted around. Sometimes, Mom and I would be in the other house while my auntie and uncle stayed somewhere else. Then everyone would transfer back to how they were before. It was the ultimate mix and match. The one constant was that those two houses were the family home base.

When the family expanded into the second house, my mom and her sister were still just kids with kids. They and my uncle were still having their fun, and the house next door became the party house. And it looked like a party house. Empty cans and bottles all over the place, which was cool with them, because they were all teenagers or just beyond. The crew they hung with would drink and smoke weed and enjoy life. At times, they would sell the weed to one another. It was never cartel-level business. Nobody was living large or moving product on the street corners. It was simply a way to make some extra cash.

My mom always had long fingernails that she took great care of and painted beautifully. People noticed them, and soon she was working hard at a shop doing other people's nails. Most in their crew had various workaday jobs. Just blue-collar living; a week-to-week paycheck kind of life. Usually making just enough to get by, but not always. Sometimes, if you sold a few ounces to your friends, it might be what it took to give you enough to feed the family or fix the car or buy the school supplies. In their world, it wasn't a big deal.

That doesn't mean that trouble never came with their selling. I remember one night when I was about nine. My mom and I were living in my Noni's house, and Auntie Agnes and Uncle Noah were staying next door with my cousin Wuv. The cops suddenly showed up at their house. Wuv burst into my room and jumped into bed with me. I asked him what was going on, but he didn't know. He was just looking for someplace safe to stay the night. The next day we found out that some guys had robbed my auntie and uncle of their drugs at gunpoint. I can't imagine they got too much. It's not like they were some big weed distribution hub. They were just young parents getting by the way the neighborhood had taught them.

As much as I loved those two houses, it was rare that I was inside them. My life was outside with my friends throwing the football, playing tag, doing all the fun, crazy stuff that kids used to do before the invention of video games. The street was my playground, and it was also my place to get away. I'm guessing there's a certain amount of dysfunction in every home. If you mix in divorce, single parenting, multiple generations, and a fair amount of partying, there are going to be times that the volume of the disagreements will crescendo. In those moments, the kids just need a place to escape. For Wuv and me, freedom was right outside our front doors.

2

STREET FAMILY

I had two families growing up. Blood gave me the first one; Maitland Avenue gave me the second.

Wuv and I were living in the two houses. Next door to the big house was our friend Hiram, and two doors down from the other house was Ruben. Across the street were Edwin and Chuck. You had to go farther down the block to get to B.J. and Paco, and past them was Miguel. Half a block from him lived Chris. These guys were the start of our pack. The bond between us was immediate and it was strong. We were always together. If you saw one of us, you saw all of us. We'd be hanging around doing all the stupid things that a group of boys does. It started in elementary school, and when junior high came along, the group grew.

We never went looking for kids to join our crew. They just did. They saw us and thought we were the kind of guys they wanted to hang with. After a while, we had guys like Frankie, Mike$ki, Big Oscar (who we also called Ketchup), Little Oscar, Chi Chi the Maui, Kellerman, TJ, Farmer Ted, Queenie, Shocker, E-Rock, Ricky Bench, Saul, Chili, and the list goes on. I would need another chapter just to call out all the homies. We were together so much that people started wondering if we were a gang. We'd be like, "We're no gang. We're just a bunch of dudes having fun."

Life with these guys was so casual, so comfortable, so easy. As we got older, we got to the age where friends from other blocks were getting jumped into gangs and finding trouble. Not us. We didn't take life that seriously. We wanted to have fun and be different. We were just chilling and enjoying the SoCal life.

Because of the strength of our numbers, we could say no to the gangs without getting harassed. For other guys, they didn't feel they had that option. The streets were pulling them in. But then they'd see us. We had the life they wanted, so they'd start hanging out. With my crew they could just be themselves and do their thing. No drama. No expectations. We kept an open door to anyone who wanted to walk in. Didn't matter who you were, what you looked like, what color you were. Homies came and went, and for the most part we always stayed cool no matter what they did.

We weren't bad kids, but we weren't churchgoers either—at least not at first. Chuck, who lived across the street, grew up in a strict Christian home. His parents loved us and always talked about Jesus, which was cool with us. We didn't have any problems with God, and we all dug Mr. and Mrs. Chuck. They were just another pair of street parents. So, if Mr. and Mrs. Chuck were cool with God, then so were we.

I was a preteen in the 1980s when my family started going to Calvary Chapel San Diego. Their youth group looked kind of cool, so the guys and I decided we'd check it out. That was a game changer for us, because we found these great older dudes there. They surfed and skated and did other cool stuff. They were the kind of guys we could look up to, almost like a big brother kind of thing. Sometimes, they'd take us on morning surf trips, or we'd go with them to youth camp. When we were together, they'd tell us, "We love God." So, we'd be like, "Cool, then I guess we love God too." Those guys showed us that we didn't need to follow the wrong ways, that it was cool to be good.

What made doing the right thing so much easier was that we had safety in numbers. It can be tough being on your own and trying to do the right thing. But with my boys, we didn't have to care what anyone else thought of us. That kind of "Screw you, we've got each other" attitude caused other kids to start noticing us. They'd say, "Yeah, they're from the neighborhood, but they love to skate and surf, and they love God." There was a respect there because they knew that even though we didn't do all the fringe things they did, we were still street kids just like them. They were Southtown; we were Southtown.

It was life with those friends that taught me to stand strong and be the guy I want to be instead of some out-of-control reprobate like everyone else expects me to be. Maitland taught me to say screw it to everyone else's expectations. You don't like me? Sorry, dude, that's a you problem, not a me one. Each of us in my crew had that freedom to say, "Yeah, I'm just going to do me," and still be accepted by the rest.

Confidence like that is attractive to people, especially to teens. Self-assurance can even make the cheesy become cool. In junior high, my friends started a surf club. Some people who knew we were going to church started mocking it, calling it Surfers for Jesus. We said, "Okay, let's run with it." We took the name, and Surfers for Jesus took off. Nothing was going to take us down. You try to label us? That's cool, we can make it work.

Once, as a joke, we decided to see if we could start a new style in high school. We started wearing our pants inside out, and soon, inside-out pants became the big fashion trend on campus. It used to be that people would rag on you if you shopped at Payless Shoes. "You're so poor your mom shops at Payless"—that kind of clowning. We decided to try another fashion experiment. There was this one cool shoe at Payless called Wallabees. So, while everyone else was wearing their crazy-expensive Reeboks and Nikes, we started wearing Payless Wallabees. Soon the whole school started wearing them, and they became the big craze in our whole area.

Maitland Avenue represents all my best friends. It's where we started life together. It's where we experienced all our firsts together—the first time we drank alcohol, the first time we tried weed, the first time we went to youth group. Unfortunately, I can all too clearly remember getting drunk for the first time. My buddy Ruben's dad, who we called Papito, built this outdoor rooftop platform, kind of like a sundeck. We decided it sounded like a great idea to spend the night on the roof and drink. Soon, we were deep into a bottle of Presidente brandy. It wasn't long before I was throwing up off the deck, letting it rain down to the ground below. Rather than getting us into trouble with our parents, Papito just said, "You're all going to learn."

I came from a broken family with a father who was usually absent, but my friends filled that gap. It didn't matter what was happening inside the four walls of the house, when I hung out with my friends, there was no drama. We could be what we wanted to be. We could do what we wanted to do. Some families are made by blood, others are made by block. That's who these guys were—my street family.

Those years of us being so tight felt like a lifetime, even though they really started just a little before seventh grade and lasted through our early twenties. But even today, my crew is still in my life. We all have our own families, and we see each other whenever, but there's a bond that cannot be broken. When things get bad for one of us, the rest gather around. They have my back and I have theirs. That's something that time can't kill.

If you're looking for Southtown, some will point you to a city or to a neighborhood. I can narrow it down to one block. Maitland Avenue is Southtown. All I needed in my life was on that street.

I WAS NINE when my mom met a new guy, John. He was good to my mom, and he took care of her. Soon, they married, and we moved into the next-door house. We were there for a couple of years. Then, in seventh grade we moved to Del Sol, which is by San Ysidro, right next to the border. That's where we stayed all through my senior year. I wasn't happy about the change of location, although now I can see how it made sense. We moved in with his parents, who were going to build onto their house for us. Back then, though, all I could see was that I was being forced to leave all my buddies.

But something as simple as distance couldn't keep us apart. When we left the next-door house, Auntie Agnes, Uncle Noah, and Wuv moved back in. Once again, all of mom's family were in one place, and family was always a magnet for her. So, even though we lived a couple miles away, we were back on Maitland just about every day. The crew survived!

When I was ten, my family expanded again. Mom had a baby girl. It was a weird time. For a decade I had been the only child. I was still getting used to having a sister when two years later Mom had another girl. That just made my Maitland Avenue family that much more important to me. I loved my sisters, and I could see how much joy they brought my mom. But between work and raising two little girls, she had her hands full. My buddies helped fill the natural gap that opened as Mom and I transitioned from just the two of us to living as a family of five.

When my homies and I hit junior high, Mom transferred me to a different school. Yeah, I wasn't thrilled about that. While all my friends went to Montgomery Middle School, I had to take the bus to Hilltop. Mom was worried that at Montgomery I'd be surrounded by a bunch of thugs and troublemakers—legitimately so. Her thinking was "better school, less trouble, more white people." Some people may not like that kind of thinking, but that's just the way it was in Southtown back then. She was looking out for me, trying to give me more opportunities.

I was miserable at Hilltop. The kids were all right, but they weren't my crew. I'd go to school in the morning, then spend every afternoon back on Maitland. No clubs, no activities other than football, nothing. Get me through classes, then get me to Maitland with my guys. When tenth grade rolled around, I was enrolled in Montgomery High School. Finally, I was back with my friends.

With Mom's remarriage, I was confronted with a new element in my life. John was white. I've always had this European skin that I got from Mom's Italian heritage. But my identity I pulled from my Islander and Mexican side. That was my Southtown culture. It's not like there were a lot of Italians living in my neighborhood.

Down in Southtown, we're a big melting pot. We've got every race, every color, every background you can think of. Even in my group of friends, we had all sorts of backgrounds. We even had some white kids. But on my block, they were the minorities.

Still, we never thought about it that way. Back then, race was never a big thing. It was something we joked about or kidded each other over. We'd say to our white buddies, "Dude, what are you doing? Quit acting so white!" They'd say stuff back to us about being Latino and we'd all laugh. Nobody worried about offending someone else. Today, people are so sensitive that everyone is walking around paranoid about saying something wrong. That's not how we rolled back then.

On Maitland Avenue, what separated us from other people wasn't the color of our skin but our economic class.

Privilege meant having money, and none of our families had it. I don't care what you look like. If you live next door to me, then we're the same. If you're in my neighborhood, then we're working through the same things, just trying to get by. If you're looking to find privilege, don't bother with skin color. Look at the bank accounts.

Again, we just never thought about race. That's why it rocked me when I was suddenly confronted with it in my new family. My mom used to do nails out of our house. One of her regular customers was Brenda Balthazar. She was this beautiful black woman, big into African culture and a counselor at Montgomery High. Miss Balthazar would be over all the time, and everyone in the house loved her.

Then one day after she left, my step-grandfather said something about her, and when he did, he dropped in the n-word. That shocked the crap out of me. I was furious. People really think this way? It floored me to hear that coming out of his mouth. At the time, I was big into reggae, and I was all about being anti-system. Suddenly, I found the oppression system was right in my house. Hearing him say that, I was seriously pissed.

I stood there trying to figure out what my family all really thought about Miss Balthazar. Were they faking it with her? Did they really look down on her, thinking that she was less of a person than they were?

I've had a lot of time over the decades to think about that incident. Quite honestly, I never would have told that story if that generation hadn't all passed on by now. What I've realized is that racism is taught. It's passed from parent to child. His words and his mindset were being filtered through a century or two of generational bigotry. It's quite possible that his grandfather or great-grandfather never would have dreamed of having the kind of normal conversations that he had with Miss Balthazar. They probably wouldn't have even let her in the house unless she was cleaning or picking up laundry.

I'm not giving him a pass for what he said. His words were inexcusable. However, I think that maybe I can give him a little redemption. Everybody has got their sinful nature. Everyone has got some kind of idiot in them somewhere. You have it. I know that I have it. When the idiot comes out, it can be ugly. And the reality is that some people's idiot can be a bit uglier than others. That day, my step-grandfather's racism idiot came out big and ugly and nasty. However, just because I may have looked at him differently from that day forward, that didn't make me stop loving him.

THE SUMMER OF MY FIFTEENTH YEAR, I started working. My stepdad had started a tile company, and he hired me on for the summer. It was hard work, but it put some cash in my pocket, and it also broadened my musical horizons. I spent most of my time listening to reggae and hip hop, but the guys on the site dropped some bands into the boom box that I hadn't heard before. Cassettes like *Join the Army* by Suicidal Tendencies and *The Record* by Fear opened my eyes to the hardcore and punk world. These influences would factor into my future big time. When I turned sixteen, I got a new job at Alpha Beta, which used to be a grocery chain in California. Finally, I was making some real money. Not a ton, but enough so that I wouldn't have to rely on anyone else.

I tried to be careful with my small paychecks. Even later in life when I made some good money, I never got into buying all the expensive stuff. I'm just a simple guy. No fancy cars. No fancy clothes. I'm a shorts, tank top, and slipper-wearing SoCal dude who dresses for comfort and not to impress a bunch of people I don't even know. I didn't buy the motorcycles and sports cars. Most of the fancy stuff I've had, I got for free.

That goes for my house too. I don't live in a mansion. I'm just tucked away in a Southtown cul-de-sac. We're not the biggest house on the block, and we're not the smallest. Inside my home, I don't bother to hang up my platinum records. The only record I have on my walls is a gold one, and that's because it matches the décor of the room. I can promise you, you can look as hard as you like—you're not going to find any Sonny shrines in my crib.

Back to Alpha Beta. For me, working was always about being independent. I wanted to meet my obligations with legit money that I earned. When I was a kid, I heard too many arguments about my dad not paying my mom child support. I can also remember those times when it seemed the month was going to last longer than the food we had in the house. I wasn't going to be the dude who put my family through that. It was that determination for self-sufficiency that kept me from going down some of the paths my friends took.

As my homies and I grew older, some of them wanted to start experimenting with this and that. We had been the mellow, cool group for a long time. We were good kids, but maybe a little too good, we thought. We were ready to start getting into a little bit of trouble. And, of course, if we were going to do it, we were going to do it together. When we wanted to try drinking, we did it as a group. When we started smoking weed, we did it as a group. But we did it in secret.

Smoking weed was a big deal back then. Those were the days when it wasn't cool to be a stoner. Most people's picture of a burner was Spicoli from *Fast Times at Ridgemont High* stumbling out of a smoke-filled van.

Those were wild times. One night we were cruising in my little Toyota truck. I had a couple guys up in the cab with me, and more were riding back in the bed. One of my friends decided to mouth off to another car passing by, and suddenly bullets started flying at us. I floored it, and we went racing down the street trying to get away from those guys. The thing is, we were laughing the whole time. Sure, it was unusual to get shot at on the street, but it was also normal in our world. Just one of the crazy things that can happen on a night out.

In the late eighties, everyone was into these big bomber sports jackets. But they were too expensive for us. So, what do you do when you really want one of those nice fancy jackets? You roll up on some dudes wearing them, beat them up, and steal their coats. I don't know how much of it was about having those jackets and how much was just this new distorted thrill and sense of power by taking them.

It seemed there was a party every weekend, and where there were parties, there were fights. Sometimes the punches would lead to some random dude pulling out a gun and taking shots. Whenever the bullets would start flying, we'd just take off running and laughing. I don't know how none of us got hit. The danger was real, but it wasn't real to us. It was almost like living in a video game. There may be bullets in the air, but they're just there to get the adrenaline pumping. They were simply part of the soundtrack of our lives.

It was around this time that Marcos Curiel, P.O.D.'s guitar player, started hanging out with my friends once in a while. In his first time with our group, he went to a party with some of the guys. Somebody popped off, which led someone else to start shooting. Marcos and my homies all took off running into a valley. My friends were cracking up, and he was like, "Dude, what is with you guys? The first time I hang out with you, and we get shot at!"

For most of the criminal stuff, I was on the outside. Again, it just wasn't my thing. I was trying to work for a living. But I didn't run away from it either. If I was around and stuff happened, then stuff happened. Still, even with some of the shadier activities that took place, it wasn't like it was scary to us. If it was my kids now and they were doing some of the crap I did, I'd be freaking out. But for us, death just wasn't something we thought about. We were invincible.

There were times when one of the guys in the group would carry a gun when we went rolling out onto the streets. One night I was in the car with some of my friends. They went driving by this dude's house, and they shot into the garage. I was like, "What the heck?" They said, "Don't sweat it, we just wanted to scare them," like it was no big deal. And for them it wasn't. And I guess for me it wasn't either, because I just laughed it off and moved on.

That's the way it was. I've always felt in the middle, being tugged by the good and the evil. All my crew knew what was right and wrong, and I was all for pushing the boundaries. But there was a limit to how far I would go. It's one thing to steal some candy at a store. Causing major hurt to people or dealing drugs, that's crossing a line that I wasn't prepared to step over. That was just my mentality. I wasn't holier than anyone else. I just had a rational mind that allowed me to think of the long-term consequences. The thought of the system locking me into a six-by-six cell? I couldn't imagine it. I'm such a free dude. I'd go crazy in a week. Doing that kind of crap just wasn't worth it. I wasn't going to be a statistic. Not a chance.

I'm not judging anybody. I'm not putting myself out there as the pious Saint Sonny proclaiming judgment on the sinful masses. I've done my share of things that would have the church moms wondering if they really should let little Kev listen to those P.O.D. thugs. Even after I had become a Christian, we'd go out to watch a show or hit a Chargers game. Someone would pop off and we'd be brawling. It wouldn't be until later that I'd be thinking, *God, what am I doing?* Actually, that's giving myself too much credit. Typically, my thoughts would be more like, *Yeah, I love Jesus and all, but these dudes swung first.*

As a guy in my teens and twenties, I had a battle with the whole "turn the other cheek" philosophy. When it came to people coming at me, I could turn the other cheek. No big deal, take your shot. But when it came to my friends and family, there was no cheek turning that was going to take place. Dude came swinging at my friends or family, and it was going to go down. I finally stopped going to house parties because every week was a fight. Even in my older years, I stopped going to Chargers games with my friends because I knew how the night would end. Everyone would start drinking, then someone would get a big mouth, then someone else would get a big mouth, then the two big mouths would start mouthing at each other and it's bleacher MMA. Probably shouldn't say this in case my kids read this book, but bleacher MMA can still be kind of fun.

Somehow, though, despite all the insanity, the crew and I managed to survive high school. Even working forty hours a week, I graduated and was planning on a quiet blue-collar life—moving up in the store, marrying my high school sweetheart, having some kids, hanging with my guys. I was all set to have exactly the life I wanted.

Then my mom got sick, and everything changed.

FULL COLOR

Sometimes you can't see it coming. You've got your plans, and they seem to be working out. Life may not be smooth, but at least you aren't having to play a constant game of "Dodge the Crisis." After high school, that's where I was. I had a direction for my life, a trajectory. If all went according to plan, within five years or so I'd be working a decent-paying blue-collar job. My high school sweetheart would be my wife, and we'd have the beginning of a family going.

But it's when you least expect it, that's when it comes. The freight train barrels in and plows through your life, and you're left wondering what the hell just happened. I've had a number of those "what the hell" experiences over the years. What I've learned is that it is in those times that I need to be looking for God the most. Because, quite often, He's the one in the engineer's cab conducting the train over me. Why does He do it? Isn't He supposed to be a God of love? He does it because most often that's the only way He can get me to stop and truly listen.

The first time the train rumbled my direction, I was completely unprepared. When it hit, it sucked the breath out of me and left me gasping. Nothing I've gone through before or since has compared. The train God was piloting shook up my entire life, and the name stenciled on the door of the engine was Aurelia.

AURELIA—THE GOLDEN ONE. It was a perfect name for my mother. She was beautiful with a cool seventies vibe. Big, curly hair, gentle, carefree spirit, into butterflies and long nails. She embodied the peace and love mentality of the era. Rarely did I hear her raise her voice; instead she looked for a quiet way out of confrontations.

Confusing her quietness for weakness, though, would be a mistake. She was a strong woman, from whom I get my stubbornness. She just wasn't an up-front, "Hey, look at me" person. She didn't need or want the spotlight. If you were looking for her, you wouldn't find her telling everyone what needed to happen. Instead, she'd be in the back getting it done herself. It's strange to say, but I got that from her also. True, I'm the guy fronting the band, jumping all around and singing to the crowd. But where I am most comfortable is backstage talking with people one-on-one, hanging out and hearing stories.

Both my mom and dad were free spirits. I think that's what drew them together. My dad and my Uncle Noah are cousins. While they were out doing their thing—partying, having fun, getting into trouble—they met these two sisters. Noah got together with the younger sister, Agnes, while my dad fell for the older, Aurelia. Although their marriage didn't last, I believe the love my mom and dad had was real.

As I talked about last chapter, Maitland Avenue was a great place to grow up. Music was a constant in the "fun house," although Uncle Noah was the only one who actually played. He was the drummer for a few local bands, gigging wherever he had a chance. He and his buddies loved making music, and I can still feel the happiness and the good times I experienced every time the instruments were out.

One great memory I have from Uncle Noah's band days was seeing my mom with her cool, homemade T-shirt. She had taken some of those old velvet, iron-on letters and pressed the band's name, "Cold Cash," down the left sleeve of a black crewneck. Across the right side of the chest, she spelled out her name. Then, in a touch that made it so much my mom, she affixed below "Aurelia" a glittery picture of a dove in the clouds surrounded by stars and a little heart with wings. It was beautiful!

In the next-door house, the vinyl rarely ceased spinning. Uncle Noah liked the more rocking stuff—Deep Purple, AC/DC, Led Zeppelin. My mom was more of a Peter Frampton and Heart kind of girl. To this day, whenever I hear the *Frampton Comes Alive* record with his amazing guitar solos and his brilliant use of the talk box, it sends me through so many different emotions.

My dad was the one who rounded out my musical experience. He was on the alternative and reggae side of the charts, and it was from him that I was introduced to

45

groups like the Police and the Pretenders and artists like Bob Marley. So, I guess you can thank him for my dreads.

I can remember when I was in eighth grade, he said, "You need to listen to this," and he put on U2's *Joshua Tree*. I was like, "Dude! This is amazing!" Between Bono's soaring vocals and the Edge's full guitar sound, it's still one of my favorite records to this day.

But my dad didn't just limit himself to one style. He could listen to an album by Jefferson Starship, then move right on to Hendrix. It was from him that I learned to love all kinds of music, even though my heart leaned toward his alternative side.

MY MOM WAS MY ONE CONSTANT all through my early life. In every memory, she figures in one way or another. Most of those recollections took place on Maitland, although at one point I'm pretty sure we lived in an apartment a small distance away. She was very involved in my life, but not like a hovering tiger mom. She was there when I needed her, and she kept her hands off when I didn't.

If my friends wanted to go skating or to hang out at Seaport Village, my mom and Auntie Agnes were always ready to drive us over. When I wanted a new skateboard or I had to have a pair of those "design them yourself" custom Vans, she'd find a way to make it happen. One day, I came home from school and there was a brand-new bed in my room. She was standing there with a huge smile on her face, so pleased that she could give me that gift. In those early years, nothing made her happier than to make me happy. She was a great mom, and I can see clearly now that she always desired the best for me. All she wanted was for me to grow up to be who I truly was.

My mom was young, beautiful, and single, and she always had a lot of good friends around her. The whole Maitland vibe was built on hanging around in a group, partying, and listening to music. Looking back, I can see a lot of the parallels between her with her friends and me with mine. We both had our crews who were like family to us. Maybe watching her was how I learned just how deep friendships could go. I'm so grateful that she had such close relationships. So much of her joy in life came from being with them.

Then, like I said, this new guy started hanging around. His name was John Silvers, and he was different than any of the other dudes she had gone out with. Younger, whiter—popping wheelies down the street on his red and white Yamaha dirt bike. Maitland Avenue wasn't really a motorcycle block; no one could really afford one. So, all my buddies and I thought John was like the second coming of Evel Knievel. His visits became more and more frequent—hanging out with the gang, having dinner with my Noni, joining in the family functions. He was a cool dude with a cool vibe. My mom had to be around twenty-six or twenty-seven, while John was just reaching the age when he could buy his first beer—only a dozen or so years older than me. But they fell in love, and soon enough they married.

I KNOW THAT FOR A LOT of kids of divorce, the family blend can be difficult. For me, though, it wasn't too bad. It wasn't like it was me and my mom against the world, and suddenly this new dude barges in and busts it up. I had my extended family and, more importantly, I had my street family. I was just glad to see my mom happy. Even when she and John had my sisters, it wasn't like I felt they were pushing me out in favor of the new shared family. Any isolation I felt from the family unit was of my own making. John was always good to me. He treated me like his own, and I knew that my mom loved him.

As I mentioned before, there came a time when we moved in with John's mom and dad. Later, his brother and his brother's wife joined us. The plan was to build onto his parents' house so that everyone could live comfortably. That would be the hub of the family tile company that they were starting. During this time, I could see in my mom's smile and her attitude that she was happy. She was entering a different chapter in her life and discovering the new her. But while she was going through those changes, I was cool staying the same old me. For that, I relied on my friends.

Thankfully, the Italian side of my mom filtered down into her excellent cooking. She learned all my Noni's recipes. But how do you outshine an Italian grandmother in the kitchen? You don't, so don't even try. Rather than focus on the pastas and the sauces, my mom exceled at baking. The creations she pulled out of her oven were ridiculous. Cream puffs, coconut cream pies, all kinds of cakes and cookies—she mastered them all.

She even made her own bread. I mean, who makes their own bread in the hood when a loaf of Wonder is like a buck-fifty down at the 7-Eleven? Certainly not any of my friends' moms. In fact, I still don't know anyone who bakes their own bread. But back then, I would come home from school, and as soon as I walked in, I could smell the dough fermenting in the bowls just waiting to be thrown into the oven. So often, I was tempted to peek under the towels to get a glimpse of the dough. I didn't dare, though, because the moment I stepped in the house, my mom warned against it. She didn't mess around when it came to baking her bread. Later, my patience would pay off when the warm, toasty, buttery scent would come wafting into my room from under my closed bedroom door.

Once the breads were out of the oven and the treats cooling on the racks, I knew that some would stay with us and some would find their way to other homes. She loved to give away her creations. I have no doubt that everyone was thrilled when they'd see her coming up the walk with gifts from her kitchen.

Once we moved in with John's family, her cooking began to change some. Their palate was different than ours. We came from a multiethnic background—an Italian world, an Islander world. Add to that my Noni working in a German restaurant, and there were all sorts of flavors going on. My Noni could cook anything from anywhere on the globe, and everything she put together was great. The background of John's family was very different. It's not that it was bad. It was just kind of, well, white. I say that with love because God knows that I love me a good burger or hot dog. Wash it down with an ice-cold can of Shasta cola and I'm yours. Still, while one side of my blended family had an eclectic mix of world flavors, the other was highlighted by canned corn and mashed potatoes. But let me tell you, my mom could mash her some Michelin star–quality potatoes!

My step-grandfather's favorite food was shepherd's pie, and my mom made a lot of those kind of basic meals. But I've got to give him and his family credit, they were always open to trying new things. When she would cook up some of the old-world recipes, they were ready with no hesitation—just as long as she kept up the regular diet of meat and potatoes and some good old mac and cheese.

John's family loved and adored my mom, and I know she felt appreciated and wanted by them. One day, being the smart-ass teen that I was, I asked her, "Why do you do all of these things for them?"

"Because I love them and they're my family," she replied.

That attitude was so very much her. If you were in her circle, you were family. When I asked her that question, I wasn't trying to be disrespectful to my mom or my new family. I just didn't want anyone to take her for granted—I didn't care who it was.

Now, when I look back, I recognize that my quiet nature made it difficult for me to really express myself to her. I didn't have the skills or know-how to tell her just how much she meant to me. As a result, I realize that the one who probably took her for granted the most back then was me.

MOM ALWAYS WORKED. For a while she was a substitute teacher, and I think there was even a stint when she took over a class for a while. But mostly I remember her doing those nails, working at a couple hip salons with friends. One look at her long, brightly polished fingernails, and women began asking her to make their nails look like hers.

This was the time of acrylics. She would have to mix the liquid and the powder, then form and shape the nails. But because she was such an artist, what my mom was really doing was creating her canvas. The airbrush had recently come on the scene. Prior to it, the "nail artists" would have to bust out the little brushes and tape off the designs. But the airbrush was a game changer, and my mom could create incredible masterpieces on the tips of her clients' fingers.

After a time, she developed a personal clientele that allowed her to start working out of the house. Friends and customers would be in and out constantly, and she was able to make some good side money. But it was more than just the money for her. She loved the relational side of doing nails. She lived for the one-on-one time when she could sit and listen to people. Sometimes she'd commiserate with them, sometimes she'd give a little advice, and sometimes she'd just stay quiet while the women let it all out.

ONCE I HIT SIXTH GRADE, I decided I wanted to try playing football. I'm not sure why. I'm not really an aggressive guy. But the opportunity presented itself and I thought, *What the heck?* I'd played more street football games than I could count, but this was the first time I tried organized ball. When I got to the practice field, they asked if I wanted to play offense or defense. The offensive side of the line is where you get to score the points, so that's what I chose.

Unfortunately, by the time I joined up, the team had already filled all the glamour positions. They were full up with quarterbacks, running backs, and wide receivers, so they put me on the offensive line. I was bummed. *Not going to score no TDs from here*, I thought. And I was right. Still, I got to be pretty good at playing guard. I wasn't really big enough for the O-line, but I had no choice but to hold my own. That's always been my attitude in life. Give me a job and I'll give it my all. I'm not looking to shine or to get the accolades. I'm just going to do my best at whatever I'm given to do.

My mother was a great football mom. She would take me to all the practices and the games, making sure that I had decent cleats and gear. When it was her turn for refreshments, she'd go to McDonald's and rent those big coolers like they use to dump Gatorade on the coaches' heads at the Super Bowl. She'd have them filled up with that McDonald's orange drink and bring them for the players. We all loved it, and everyone thought Moms was cool because she hooked us up with the Hi-C.

Throughout my Pop Warner football stint, the name "Silvers" was on the back of my jersey. The coaches even called me "Silvers." I didn't think anything of it at the time, but later it struck me as unfortunate. There was nothing malicious about it, but I'm a Sandoval. I sometimes wonder how my dad must have felt when he saw me with another guy's name on my back.

Football jumped to the next level when you hit tenth grade. Pop Warner and high school ball were two different things. Suddenly, there were tryouts to make the team, and the coaches wanted everyone to practice during the summer. I was like, *Yeah, that ain't happening.* Can you blame me? Summer is for surfing and for hanging. It's not for running two-a-days out in the SoCal sun. So, I ditched the practices. Instead, I spent the summer hopping the bus in the mornings, riding it to the beach, surfing and messing around until evening, then riding home.

We didn't have cell phones in those days. Our parents had no way to catch up with us. We'd just say bye in the morning, then we'd be home in time for dinner. I can't imagine doing that with my kids today. I've got to know where they are all the time. I don't know if the world's gotten crazier or if we're all a lot more paranoid.

It was a great summer. When school started, I figured my football days were over. But I think the coach must have been short some warm bodies for the team. He'd heard that my buddies and I played, so he came and asked us to join up. We figured why not? We get to play football, but we didn't have to give up our summer. Win-win!

The varsity roster was full, so he threw us onto the JV team. This time I was determined to play defense. I was tired of running headfirst into dudes who had fifty pounds on me. After a couple practices, the coach started me at strong safety. I was stoked. Rather than colliding with the monsters on the O-line, I got to tackle fools—which is always fun.

I was hyped for the season, but during the first game I sprained my wrist. I don't know what it was, but something clicked inside me. Suddenly I was done with football. Later, when the coach asked me if I was ready to play again, I said, "Nah, I'm good." And that was the end of the storied Sandoval football career. Thinking about it now, I wish I would've stayed on the team and continued to varsity the next two years. But I was just having way too much fun with my friends to commit to a sport that would interfere with our time together.

Or maybe it was something else. Could it have been something deeper in my psyche that caused me to not want to make that kind of commitment? I remember when Wuv and our buddy Chuck started taking karate with one of our youth leaders, and they wanted me to join. I was like, "No thanks. Not interested." Was I just scared that I wouldn't be good at it? Am I that afraid of failure? Or maybe it was all just part of me figuring out who I was. Maybe there was this musical something or other that God had created in me that I hadn't discovered yet. It could have just been that I had to try a few things until the right one fit, like trying on jeans until you find the perfect pair. Seems to me that's a lot of what being a teenager is all about.

SOMETIME AROUND MY MOM'S MARRIAGE to John, my Uncle Noah and Auntie Agnes started going to church. Soon after, their lives began changing. The partying stopped, and at their house I saw my uncle hosting Bible studies. Even as a kid I could see that something was going on. Every now and then, I'd join them for church and go to Sunday school. I can't remember exactly when my mom began going, but soon she was a regular too.

I liked their church because it was different than what I was used to. Like many good Italian families, we would go to Catholic mass on Easter and Christmas Eve. I liked the Christmas Eve midnight mass, because when we'd get home around 1:00 a.m. we'd get to open our presents.

The Calvary Chapel that my uncle and auntie went to was very different from that traditional feel. First, it was a whole lot louder. People were singing and clapping and really getting into the music. When the pastor would preach, he would make jokes, and we wouldn't get frowned at for laughing. Instead of a fancy building, they met in an office complex. Instead of a big ceramic Jesus hanging on a cross at the front of the church, they just had the name "Jesus" in big letters. Nobody was sad. Nobody seemed angry. Everyone was just having a good time.

If it seems like I'm slamming the Catholic church, then you're reading me wrong. I'm just telling you how I viewed it as a kid. My Noni is Catholic through and through. I remember when I was little walking into her room with her big Jesus and Mary statues on her nightstand and all her rosaries surrounding them. I swear they must have been at least three feet tall. It felt like I was on hallowed ground—the holy prayer room. There was a reverence to it. Catholicism is what she was raised with. It's how she feels she can worship and honor God the best. I'm not about to tell a modern-day saint that she needs to change so she can worship more like me.

The "church" changes in my mom were subtle. She had always been a caring, loving, good-natured person. Christianity brought with it peace and contentment she hadn't necessarily had before. It fit with her desire to rebuild her family. Once my stepdad, John, became a Christian also, God was put right in the middle of the family mix.

For me, what made church great was that my friends would come too. We pretty much took over the youth group and had a great time with the leaders. I guess I thought I was a Christian at that time, but I don't think I really knew what being a Christian was.

I remember when I was a kid in elementary school, I was standing on the sidewalk with my buddy Chuck. He was the friend I mentioned who had two charismatic Christians for parents.

Chuck asked me, "Dude, do you love Jesus?"

Well, who doesn't? I said, "Of course I love Jesus."

"Do you want to receive Him into your heart?"

"Of course!" *I mean, who wouldn't?*

So, he led me in this prayer that I'm sure he had overheard at church. I repeated his words, and—boom!—suddenly I was a Christian. At least I thought I was. I may not have understood what I was praying, but I felt good because at least I said the words. I hung on to that prayer for a lot of years, until the time came that I was faced with the decision as to whether I really believed what I had said or not.

WHEN MY SENIOR YEAR came around, I was already working forty hours a week at an Alpha Beta grocery store. I had earned enough credits so that I didn't need a first period, and the school gave me a work permit that allowed me to leave by noon. It was a busy year, but a good one. A little bit of school, a whole lot of work, and the rest of the time I spent hanging with my girlfriend, Shannon, and my friends.

The September after I graduated, I started a couple classes at Southwestern Community College. It's not like I had any great educational goal in mind. I just figured it couldn't be a bad thing. I was all set for a good year.

Then my mom got sick. She went to the hospital, and they ran a whole bunch of tests on her. I was sitting with my mom and my stepdad when the doctor came in and told her she had cancer. Leukemia.

I can remember her asking the doctor, "What did I do? How did I get it?"

He answered, "You didn't do anything. Sometimes it just happens."

That's the suck of this world. *Sometimes it just happens.*

I don't know what's worse. Smoking a couple packs a day and ending up with lung cancer or getting hit by the bad luck of the draw. With one, you've only got yourself to blame, but at least there's someone to point a finger at. With the other, the only answer you have is it sucks to be you.

This many years later, I can't tell you at what stage her cancer was at that point or any of the details. I just know that it was bad. They put her on a very aggressive chemo, and all that beautiful curly hair of hers fell out. And she got horribly sick. I remember all of us getting tested to see if we had the right blood cells or bone marrow that we could give to her, but none of us were a match. That was one more punch to the gut.

It was rough—for her and for all of us. Everyone had to step up. The house still had to be taken care of. My sisters still needed to be watched. Physically and emotionally, it wiped us out. But more than anyone else, my mom suffered day after day after day.

But the chemo worked.

After months of treatment, my mom got the word that the cancer had gone into remission. You want to talk about a party! You can't imagine the celebration! She had beaten it!

I can't say that I was surprised, though. That was how life was supposed to work. You're sick, you get treatment, you get better. I'd had friends die before but in accidents or as the result of some kind of violence. Once, a homie of ours was shot and killed just pulling onto the freeway. That was how you died. I'd never really accepted that my mom might not pull through. First, she was way too young to die of an old people's disease. But mainly because when you get sick, you take medicine, and you get better.

And I was right. That's what happened. All the stress fell off my shoulders. It was time to have fun again. I had quit the community college when my mom first got sick, so I didn't have that eating up my time anymore. It just meant that much more opportunity to hang with my homies.

A FEW MONTHS LATER, my mom was feeling just a little off. That wasn't unusual. Her body had taken quite a beating. She went to go get checked out like she had done other times before. But instead of releasing her, the doctors admitted her, saying they wanted to run a few more tests. I wasn't tripping over that. Doctor visits and overnight stays had become part of her routine. It was business as usual.

She ended up staying longer than normal. Then one night while she was posted up at the hospital, I had the chance to go to a punk show and let off some steam. After the show, me and the crew went to my boy Paco's house. This was our typical after-show routine. Get our party on and have a smoke session. I was expecting my usual good time, but this night I was all locked up in my head. I kept feeling like something wasn't right. I ended up sitting there all night just kind of bad tripping.

The next day, I wasn't in the mood for another visit to the hospital. I didn't like hospitals then, and I definitely hate them now. I called up my stepdad, John, and made an excuse for why I couldn't make it down there. He was more than understanding and told me not to worry about it.

Not long after I hung up, my pager buzzed. I didn't recognize the number, so when I called it, I asked, "Who's this?"

"Hey, this is Auntie," said my dad's sister, Auntie Uilani. "You need to get down here."

I was like, "Why? What's up?"

"I'm at the hospital. You just need to get here now."

When I walked into my mom's room, I saw a completely different person. I'd never seen her look so bad. She was shivering and shaking. I freaked out. I went to her bed and leaned down next to her.

"Hey, son," she said.

Those were the last words she ever said to me.

I stayed with her through the night, and she deteriorated rapidly. By the next morning, she had lost consciousness and was unresponsive. Nobody quite knew what was going on, including the doctors.

This was so unexpected that I wasn't sure what to do. Looking back now, I think I had a mixture of shock and "I've got to be strong for my family" going on. I did my best to keep my emotions locked away. I couldn't allow myself a breakdown.

My mom survived the day. And the next day. And the next. At the start of each day, the doctors would come in and say, "Prepare yourselves. She won't make it through the day." At the end of the day, she would prove them wrong again. So, the doctors came back in the evening and said, "Prepare yourselves. She won't make it through the night."

It was so hard to watch her in that bed. They had her all hooked up with tubes and wires. In the beginning, she would have these uncontrollable bouts of shivering. We'd heat up blankets in the microwave and lay them over her to warm her up. Eventually, everything shut down. She was comatose.

I never left. I stayed in her room day after day. This was my mom. She was my world.

Then one morning, the doctor came in, and he said something different from his usual "Prepare yourself" speech.

He said, "You know, what I'm about to tell you isn't a medical term. But around here, we have something we call Mother's Heart. It may be that your mother doesn't want to die, because she doesn't want to leave her kids behind."

That hit me like a fist.

My mind went back to a conversation I'd had with my mom not long before she'd gone back to Zion Medical Center. I was trying to sneak into the house so that she couldn't see I was high. But she was waiting for me at the bottom of the staircase. There was no way for me to get to my bedroom without crossing her path. I remember her looking up at me and saying, "Sonny, you've lost your first love."

I wasn't exactly sure what she meant, but then she said, "I don't want to die without knowing for sure that you're going to be with me in heaven."

That kind of surprised me. I wasn't really a bad kid. I was no rebel. Sure, I was making some bad decisions every now and then like every teenage guy that's ever lived. But as I sat in that chair in her hospital room, I realized that she had been saying more to me than just, "Son, be good." She was much more concerned that I was right with God than she was that I was right with her.

And all I could think of was that she had the power to let go, but she was hanging on because of me. She could leave this life and end the pain and be with her Jesus in heaven, but instead her love for me kept her suffering in that bed.

My family could see that I was all messed up after hearing the doctor's words. They told me to go home and get cleaned up. Take a shower, change out of the clothes I'd been wearing since the night I arrived at the hospital. I agreed and left the room.

When I got to my '91 Chevy Cavalier, though, everything hit me. Without a doubt, my mom was going to die.

There was no stopping that. The best thing that could happen would be for it to take place sooner rather than later. End the suffering now. But it was very possible that I was the reason that she was still hurting. All I ever wanted was for her to be happy. Instead, I was causing her to experience suffering and agony.

Sitting in my car, stunned, heartbroken, pissed off, I started talking with God. "I don't know what I'll do if my mom dies. God, I don't know what I'm going to do without her. But I don't want her suffering like this. So, I'll make a deal with you. I don't want all that religion. I hate that stuff. I don't want the blue-eyed, blond-haired Jesus. I don't want the convert-or-else God of the crusades or any of the TV, holy water, flopping on the ground preachers. I want my mom's Jesus. If that's who You are—if You're truly my mom's Jesus—then I'll follow You because that's the only way I'm going to make it through this. And I think that's the only way she's going to let go."

Then I went back to some of that prayer that I prayed with Chuck all those years before. But this time I really understood what I was saying. I prayed, "I know that I'm a sinner. And I know that You're a God who forgives sins. I believe You want to save me and change me just like You've done with my family. If I can have the Jesus who gave my mom that peace and contentment, then I'll follow You 100 percent."

I went home and got cleaned up. When I got back to the hospital, I walked up to the side of the bed and I whispered in my mom's ear, "Go and be with Jesus. Your girls and I are going to be all right."

PEOPLE CAME IN FROM ALL OVER. The hospital room was packed, and we had pretty much taken over the waiting room. Even my dad's brother, Uncle Tony, came to be with the family. I think it was getting too crowded, so the adults sent some of us younger ones out to get food. We went down to the car, and my girlfriend Shannon and I got in the back seat. Up front was Wuv and someone else—I can't remember who.

As we drove out of the parking lot, I turned to Shannon and said, "Wait, what am I doing? I can't leave my mom again."

But she calmed me down and said, "It'll be okay. We need to go."

I can't really remember the drive or even where we went. All I can remember is pulling back into the hospital parking lot. My Uncle Tony was outside smoking a cigarette, and he was shaking his head. Immediately, I knew what that meant. Wuv and I jumped out of the car and went running into the hospital.

When we made it to the right floor, the world got really weird. I mean freaky weird. Even thinking about it now creeps me out. It was like a Matrix moment where it felt like the hall stretched out and I was moving in slow motion. Picture Neo dodging the bullets—that was me trying to get to the room. My mind was working in real time, but I could feel the movement of my surroundings slowing down. I could see and hear everything around me. I could smell that damp, antiseptic hospital scent. But it was like I wasn't fully present. I still hate hospitals today because they remind me of that freaky vibe I experienced.

When I finally exited my Matrix moment and made it to her room, I could see all my family members crying. I ran to the bed and wrapped her lifeless body in my arms. I knew that others were around, but I wouldn't let go. I can remember that her mouth kept falling open, so I had to hold it closed for her. I don't know exactly what happened in that time, but soon they were telling us that we needed to go. It felt like it had been only minutes, but when I finally looked up at that standard white three-handed clock hanging in the top center of the wall, I realized I had been holding her for hours. I got up, looked toward the door, and walked out.

As I left the hospital, I spotted my dad. I went up to him, and he talked to me for a while. He told me that it was time for me to be a man. It wasn't in a negative way, but more of a "You've got this, son. You can handle this." He probably doesn't know how much that meant to me.

I didn't tell anyone about my conversation with God in the parking lot until the day of my mom's funeral, when I talked with my Uncle Noah. I let him know that before my mom died, I gave my life to Jesus.

Truthfully, it was a proud moment for me. It was me saying to him, "I'm ready for God to change my life. I'm going to be all in, like you." At that moment, he was the only person I was ready to share that with, and he, too, probably doesn't know just how much that meant to me.

My mom dying so young was a tragedy. But it's also an amazing story about how incredible God is. My mom would have done anything for me. In a heartbeat, she would have given up her life. And, in a sense, that's what she did. It was through her death that I found eternal life.

I have no doubt that for my mom that was a fair trade. You wouldn't have to ask her twice. How do I know? Because I'd do the same for my kids.

I don't know how many times my mom must have prayed for me. She knew that in His time, God would answer her prayers. Once I could tell her that I was okay with Jesus and she could go be with her Savior, she was able to finally let go, knowing that God had been faithful—literally, to her last breath.

NOTHING TO LOSE

My mom's funeral was packed. The officials running the service said that it was the most people they'd ever had at a memorial. Family, current friends, people from back in the day stood around her graveside. It was a testament to who she was that so many wanted to come and show their love and pay their respects. Afterward, everyone migrated to my Noni's house to hang out, tell stories, and eat some of her cooking.

Once my mom was laid to rest, I went back to business as usual, trying to lose myself in my routine. I kept thinking that there had to be a reason for it. Who dies of cancer at thirty-seven? Seriously. God had to be in there somewhere with some plan, but I just wasn't seeing it. It's not that I was pissed at Him. So many people get angry at God and blame Him when bad things happen. But I figure that if we trust in His love in the good times, then we need to do the same in the tough times. I knew that somehow this would make sense eventually. In the meantime, I'd live up to my end of the bargain I struck with God.

First thing that I did was to look at my life. It used to be that I was a functioning stoner. I'd be cashiering at the grocery store. When my lunch break came, I'd go smoke with my friends. Then, I'd come back and finish my shift. Everything was cool. But when I made this commitment to God, I knew this was something I had to change. It wasn't like, "Dude, I suck as a person if I'm lighting up all the time." I just knew there were some things that would get in the way of me getting close to God, and this was one of them. No surprise that my friends had my back as I looked to drop getting high from my life. Whatever journey I was going to walk, they'd be there to support me, even if they weren't walking the same path themselves.

REWIND THE TAPE A FEW YEARS to high school. My cousin Wuv was playing drums in a thrash band called Eschatos with Marcos Curiel and two other dudes, Andre and Gabe. Despite their music being a little harder than what I was into, my buddies and I were always going to their shows because they were part of the crew. We wanted to be around to see them play. We also wanted to be close so we could step in if something popped off. The more I went, the more I started getting into it. Everyone would be moshing and pitting, slamming into each other and just getting crazy. I loved it. It was a great release to jump in the pit and get all aggressive, dominating and pushing people around.

But even more than just the adrenaline release of being at their gigs, there was something seriously cool about those dudes. This was a time when it seemed that every band stood for something. There were the straight edge bands, the vegans, the Krishnas; everyone had their cause. Eschatos was made up of four cool, young Christian guys who weren't afraid to let everyone know what they believed while they were thrashing it out. They weren't out to convert anyone who came to their shows. But they weren't going to be intimidated to shut up about their faith either. I admired that about them.

To me, they were a different kind of Christian band. I knew about Stryper and Deliverance and other bands who were mostly making music for the church kids. And that's cool if that's what they felt called to do. More power to them. There were even a few Christian kids I knew who could get down with the best of us. But Wuv and Marcos and the guys just wanted to play, and they didn't want to be confined to church basements and youth retreats. That's when I discovered the difference between Christian bands and bands that are made up of Christians.

I dug the sound of Eschatos, but it wasn't my main vibe. I was into reggae and rap. A few of my buddies also loved to rap and we'd get together to hang and freestyle. I never had any intention of being in a rap group, although at one point my close buddies Chris and Rick wrote some lyrics, came up with a cool rap group name, and Unlicensed Product was born. We might have even recorded a song with the homie DJ Mike$ki, but I can't really remember. So, I guess technically it was possible we were an official rap group for one summer.

But it was just fun to me. It was never going to be my future. I'm not the up-front dude. I don't want to be in the spotlight. We'd go to a party and all the others would get this rap circle going, and I'd just stand there and let them go. Besides, I already had my life planned out—marry Shannon, move up in the grocery store, have some kids, live a good life down in Southtown.

Right around the time my mom died, Wuv and his band started thinking they wanted to go in a different direction. There was this San Diego straight edge band called House of Suffering. They had a great sound, mixing a cool heavy groove with rap vocals. The Eschatos guys had already discussed Marcos Curiel stepping down from the vocals so he could focus on his guitar, so now they started talking about who they could put in his place.

"What do you think about Sonny?" Wuv asked. "He's in that rap group."

Marcos just laughed. "Sonny? He barely even talks to me." He didn't say this to be a jerk. He was just thinking, if Sonny hardly talks to anyone, how is he going to front a band? Totally fair question!

It wasn't until years later that Wuv admitted that he had his doubts too. But he thought, *Auntie Aurelia just died, and maybe Sonny needs something new to get him out of his own head*. So, they came to me and said, "Hey, we're starting up a new band. What do you think about being the front man?"

My first reaction was, "That's not me." It was awesome to be asked, and I was stoked at what they were trying to do as a band. But a front man I am not.

Still, I'd been around Christians long enough to know what I was supposed to say: "Thanks, guys. Let me pray about it."

NOT LONG AFTER MY MOM PASSED, I started working the night crew at the grocery store. It was a promotion, and I've always been kind of a night guy. During one shift, one of my managers came to me and said, "Sonny, why don't you take a couple weeks off? You have the paid vacation. Use it and get away." I appreciated that they cared enough to see I needed some time to get my head together. I thanked them and took the weeks.

At that time, my Uncle Noah was doing landscaping with In-N-Out Burger, and Wuv was working with him. They were crisscrossing the palm trees and making the properties look pretty. Uncle Noah was sent up to a new restaurant in Fresno, and he asked me to come along during my time off from the store. It was hard work, but it was good to get away.

Wednesday night came, and we decided to hit up the midweek service at Calvary Chapel Fresno. While we were waiting for it to kick off, two other dudes came in. One of the big California hardcore thrash bands of the time was The Crucified, and as we watched, Jim Chaffin, the drummer, and Jeff Bellew, the bassist, walked down the aisle. We had seen them play a bunch of times, and Wuv and I were tripping out that these guys were here in this church.

After the service, we went up to them and started talking. They were amazingly kind and generous with their time.

Wuv told them about his band and that they were trying to do some different things. Then, he told them that he was trying to get me to join up. Meanwhile, I'm taking the whole thing in. To us, these guys were big time. And to see them at church was just a beautiful thing. They could pound out their sound while remaining authentic to their faith. They were rockers, yet they could still be on fire for God.

That night when we got back to the Motel 6, I told Wuv, "Dude, I think the band is something I'm supposed to do." He was psyched, and we immediately started writing lyrics. That night we inked out our first song, "Three in the Power of One." It eventually ended up on our demo and our first album, *Snuff the Punk*. I listen to that song now and think, *Dude, it's so cheesy!* But we were just kids. The song was from the heart, and it was real.

The rest of the time we were in Fresno, I'd spend my evenings listening to Eschatos demos and adding my own lyrics to the songs. I was no poet. I'd never taken a creative writing course. I just started writing. I wrote about God. I wrote about life. I wrote about whatever came into my mind that seemed to fit the feel of the jam the band had laid down. The creativity was flowing, and I was loving it.

WHEN WE GOT BACK FROM FRESNO, we met up with the band formerly known as Eschatos. At that time, it was Marcos Curiel on guitar, Wuv Bernardo, my cousin, on drums, and Gabe Portillo on bass. Our buddy Andre wouldn't be joining this jam session since the guys didn't feel a need to have two guitar players. We set up in the living room of

Gabe's grandma's house, mic'd my vocals through whatever ghetto bass cabinet we had at the time, and started trying it out.

Because we were already friends—all part of the crew—there was no awkward, trying-to-prove-ourselves-to-the-others period. We were buddies with a history. They were used to jamming together, and I just worked on seeing where I could fit in. I loved doing the rap stuff. But it was a big step for me to come out and try to sing and scream. It took me a while to get comfortable with letting it all go like that. In fact, I'm still trying to get totally comfortable with it thirty years later.

Now that we had a new band, we needed a new name. We wanted it to be hard and to sound different from everything else that was out there. There were a ton of single-name bands at the time—Metallica, Sepultura, Nirvana, Pantera. We wanted multiple words, a name that would stand out from the rest. So, we were throwing out idea after idea and shooting them down one after another. Nothing fit.

Then Wuv's girlfriend at the time pitched in an option. She was working at a bank and said that when someone who has a will dies, all their money, valuable assets, and other stuff that they intended to give away are considered "Payable on Death." It was beautiful. It was heavy and tough, and it perfectly related to Christ paying for our sins, so that through Him we could have eternal life.

So, we became Payable on Death, and we started gigging around Southtown and up in San Diego. It didn't take long, though, to realize why there were so many single name bands out there. Saying Payable on Death multiple times at every show was a mouthful and got old fast. We decided that three letters were better than three words, and shortened it to the acronym P.O.D.

Our first real gig was at a local venue called SOMA. Their main auditorium held a couple thousand people, and they would bring in all these cool, big-name acts. However, they had a second stage down in the basement. The Dungeon held only a little more than a hundred people, and on weeknights they would let local bands and lesser-known groups play there.

The deal with The Dungeon was if any band was able to bring in at least one hundred people who said their name when they bought their tickets, Len Paul, the owner, would put them on the main stage for a weekend gig. The guys and I decided we had to get in on that action. We got the word out to all our families, our friends and homies, and the neighborhood, and we packed the place out. Len was impressed, not just that we filled the venue, but that we killed our set. He told us that he'd find a place for us on the main stage.

A little time passed, then Len gave us a call. He told us that Green Day was playing the New Year's Eve show. This was before the band had signed with Reprise Records, but they were already huge. Someone had fallen off the bill for the show, and Len invited us to take their slot. We jumped at it, going nuts that our second real venue gig was opening for Green Day.

P.O.D. STARTED TO MAKE SOME NOISE in the San Diego area. We still played house parties and the like, but we were getting more and more dates at clubs and music venues. About eight months in, we got a primo gig at the world-famous Whisky a Go Go in Los Angeles. Rob Halford had just left Judas Priest and was launching his own band, Fight. P.O.D. signed to open for him. We were stoked.

Then Gabe dropped a bomb on us. He just wasn't feeling the band anymore. Our music was aggressive and heavy. Gabe was more of a punk guy. He said he was ready to do something different.

We were freaking out. There was no way we were going to miss playing at the famous Whisky, opening for a legend like Rob Halford, but how could we play without a bassist? Then we had a thought. My Uncle Sal was in a funk band, and their bass player, Traa Daniels, was the best we knew. Problem was that he was a funk and jazz guy. Still, we were desperate. We called up Uncle Sal and asked, "Hey, can you ask Traa if he would come and jam with us so that we don't miss this show?"

Traa agreed and started practicing with us. The connection was immediate. He is so good, and he brought an incredibly cool new vibe. We played the show, then afterwards asked him, "Dude, what do you think about being part of the band?" He was in and quit my Uncle Sal's band. I still feel a little bad about that. Sorry, Uncle Sal.

The addition of Traa was perfect for P.O.D. Marcos was big into metal. Wuv loved metal, but he also was more of a jazz guy. Traa had his funky Earth, Wind & Fire, old-school R&B vibe. I loved rap and reggae but still enjoyed my doses of punk. Four different guys from four different musical spectrums, but when we got together, it somehow blended. Just like Southtown with its melting pot of ethnic groups, we were a melting pot of music. P.O.D. didn't fit into an existing genre. We made up our own. And people dug it.

This beautiful blend fit perfectly with my musical journey. Like I said earlier, my parents and my environment helped expose me to different styles and sounds growing up. But by the time I hit middle school, I was all about rap and reggae. It fit my rebel attitude and it fit my Islander background. In my young mind, I had musical styles divided all by ethnicity. Metal and punk were for the white kids. If you were black, you liked hip hop and R&B. That's just the way it was, I thought. When I'd see these white kids with their leather and their spiky hair, I'd think, "Why would I like their music? That's not me. I've got nothing in common with them."

Then one day I discovered Bad Brains. Four black dudes playing punk rock music. It blew my mind. Then I heard Suicidal Tendencies and saw a Mexican guy and a black guy from Venice Beach doing punk. Why were they playing white music when they're not white? Suicidal Tendencies was from the street just like me, and when I saw them with their bandanas and their cholo mentalities, I was thinking these guys look like they could be *eses* from the hood. It was a revelation to me. I realized that music for me didn't have to be just reggae or hip hop, or the AC/DC and Led Zeppelin that I grew up with. There was a whole untapped world of styles that I wanted to explore. The eclectic direction that P.O.D. took musically was a perfect fit for where I'd been the past six or seven years.

I WANT TO BACKTRACK just a bit. Soon after P.O.D. launched and we started getting some gigs, we knew we needed a demo. It was the next logical step. If we wanted to book more venues or get people to hype the band word-of-mouth, we needed something to put into their hands. My Uncle Noah, Wuv's dad, set it up for us. He believed in the band and wanted to see us hit. So, he became our unofficial manager, checking out the venues, making sure they were set with the right equipment, doing everything he could to make sure his son's and nephew's band had the best chance at succeeding. In those early days, he was indispensable.

Woody Barber worked at Sounds West Studio, and Uncle Noah set us up with him. Woody had a big name in the San Diego scene and was an excellent engineer. It made me feel like a rock star sitting in that big open recording room with the tape rolling. Then it was my turn to sing in front of everybody. Talk about nerve-racking. I sat there with my headphones on, and suddenly I'm hearing my voice clearly for the first time. Nobody likes their voice when it's played back to them. Thirty years later, I still have a hard time listening to myself sing. And I knew that as bad as I thought I sounded, everyone else wearing cans over their ears was hearing the exact same thing.

To add to the stress, this was the analog era of tape. Nothing was digitized. You couldn't simply retake a vocal and punch it in. If I screwed up, I'd have to start all over again. Recording to tape was a tedious process and hugely intimidating.

On the A side of our cassette were four tracks, and on the B side we dropped six more. Most of the songs would find their way onto our first album. The cardboard tucked into the plastic case was black with big red block letters "P.O.D." Below that was written "Payable on Death." We were stoked at how it turned out. Everybody who would take one got one. We were passing them out to strangers, selling them at our gigs, anything we could do to create a buzz. The reaction was great, especially down in Southtown—"Hey, check the homies' cassette tape!" But the fact was that it was just a demo tape done on a demo budget. Soon, it came time to put some high-quality sounds onto a real record.

The difference between our demo and our first album, *Snuff the Punk*, was huge. We had evolved as a band, and we also now had Traa with his slapping, funk bass. Jeff Bellew, bassist for The Crucified, heard we were cutting a record, and he came down to help produce. We were blown away. This was a professional rock star with an established band, and he's coming down to help us cycle through our songs. And he was going to put his name on it!

I was just as uncomfortable when it came time to record the album as I was cutting the demo. Even though I now had some experience under my belt playing live shows and developing my own style, it was still me listening to myself through those damn headphones. But I was recording with my boys. Any criticism I was feeling was only coming from myself. We weren't just a band; we were family. I think that's always come through in our music.

Quite honestly, when I listen to *Snuff the Punk* now, I cringe. We were nineteen-year-old kids—so young and immature. My lyrics were cheesy and over the top. It was like, "Dude, I'm a Christian! So, what's up! You got a problem with that?" They're just so green.

Our album cover was a perfect illustration of our in-your-face attitude. On a black background, there's this crazy-looking assassin angel-type thing. He's got the devil in a headlock with a gun pointed at his head. Satan is grabbing at his arm and has his tail wrapped around the pistol, trying to pull it away. It was hard, edgy, and scary as hell.

If you've got the album, you may be thinking, *Sonny, dude, I think you're mixed up. The cover of* Snuff the Punk *has an angel with a huge fist about to punch the devil's lights out.* You're not wrong. What's throwing you off is that you have a copy of the album's 1999 reissue. That's after the album got busted by the Bible bookstore execs who felt that having a gun on the cover was too hardcore for little Timmy to see in the record rack. That was the first of our numerous cover issues over the years.

I WORE MY CHRISTIANITY like a chip on my shoulder, daring anyone to come knock it off. For a while, I didn't even see P.O.D. as me being in a band; it was my ministry. Again, I can't blame the young me. I didn't know better. I thought we were doing it the holy, Christian way. Over time we grew up, gained some wisdom, and learned how to express ourselves without leaving anyone feeling like they just got punched in the gut.

For instance, on that first album we had a song called "Abortion Is Murder." Partway through the song, we break into a chant singing the title phrase over and over—eight times. Later, we pick up the chant again. I am as pro-life as it comes. I believe that life begins at conception. But, holy crap, even I cringe at those lyrics.

I'll never forget a guy who sent a letter to Rescue Records. Actually, let me pause here a second. *Snuff the Punk* was released on Rescue Records. The problem was that Rescue Records didn't exist yet. We wanted to be able to say we had a label so we could look big time, so we put the name on the album. All credit to my Uncle Noah who came up with the name, then afterwards created an independent label under that name and used it to launch a bunch of cool new acts.

So, this Christian dude sent a letter. He was a musician, an acoustic guy who played coffee shops. He was like, "I've been following you guys. I'm excited for you, and I love your zeal." Good so far. He went on, "If I could give you just one piece of advice. You're gaining in popularity, and you're playing places that I could never play. They're places that most guys who are vocal about their faith never get into. Don't forget to lead in love. Remember, you are guests in the world's house, and you want them to invite you back. Leave the self-defense behind, and lead in love."

Lead in love.

That was quite possibly the best piece of advice I've ever received when it comes to the band. We were so militant, so preachy. What about the girl who may have recently had an abortion? Maybe she was coming to our concert just to get away from the struggles of her life. Maybe she was longing to hear a little hope. Instead, she heard me chanting, "Abortion is murder! Abortion is murder!" Dude, it breaks my heart to even think about that possibility.

Every album tells a story. For me, *Snuff the Punk* tells the story of me trying to figure out who I am. I was searching for my lyrical style. I was trying to find my hard voice. I was looking for who I was as a Christian who had been given a platform. It was part of my life timeline—like a chapter in a book. Taken by itself, *Snuff the Punk* was just a random hardcore album made by a bunch of kids. Taken in context, it was the necessary first step on the P.O.D. journey.

5

WE REALLY DOING THIS?

Even though *Snuff the Punk* was only released on cassette, word of this rap, hardcore San Diego band started spreading outside of California. Meanwhile, we were still trying to figure out how this whole band thing worked. All we knew up to that point was play shows, hustle tapes, and sell whatever merch we could. Nice thing about being based in the bottom-left corner of the US was that we could easily cross the border to Tijuana to get the best deals on T-shirts, hats, and beanies.

Before we knew it, we found ourselves with an invitation to play the new band stage at Cornerstone '94. Started a decade earlier, the Cornerstone Festival was the place to play if you were a Christian band. Held in a field in hot and humid western Illinois around the beginning of July, the five-day festival was crowded, sweaty, and dirty. But anybody who was anybody in contemporary Christian music wanted to be there.

I've got to admit, when we got the invite, I had no clue what Cornerstone was. We were still so green to the Christian music industry. But we figured, a spot at a big festival with thousands of people attending? That's where it's at.

As great as it was to be asked to Cornerstone, it was another thing to get there. Bushnell, Illinois, was almost two thousand miles away, and none of us were making much money at that time. Then we got a call from a new Christian hardcore punk band called The Blamed. We had met those guys playing shows around town. They were also heading to Cornerstone and had booked some gigs along the way. They were like, "Hey, let's team up together." So we tossed our equipment into my buddy's truck, piled into a rented Astro van, and took off across the country.

Those concerts we played along the way were eye-opening. All our previous gigs had been in and around California. We knew that scene. But now we were discovering that there were like-minded people in other states too. We'd set up in the basement of a church, and soon the room would fill up with tattoos and mohawks and dyed hair—all the stuff that we were getting flak for back in Cali. And these cultural rebels all loved God, just like we did. And they loved to praise Him very loudly—again, just like we did.

When we arrived at the festival, we found more of the same. It opened our eyes that not only were there a lot of bands out there like us, but there were a lot of Christians that had the same mentality. They, too, were loudly and, at times, aggressively glorifying God. It was validating. It let us know that we weren't just lone rebels against the buttoned-up Christian traditions, but we were part of a valid subculture within the true church. If people didn't like it, they were more than welcome to go sing their hymns up in the sanctuary. We'd keep praising God our way down in the basement.

Our set at Cornerstone was a trip. We were in one of those circus-looking tents packed with a sweat-soaked, highly aggressive crowd just waiting to let out some excess energy. I don't know what the temperature was in there, but I do remember telling the audience that if one of us passed out, they should just stand us back up and we'd keep going. We opened singing a praise chorus that was popular at the time, then broke into "Coming Back." The place went crazy. For a lot of them, that was the only song of ours that they knew, having heard it on a Tooth & Nail compilation album.

Tooth & Nail Records was a California label founded in 1993 by a guy named Brandon Ebel. He saw the power of the Christian punk and hardcore scene and wanted to get it out to the masses. Soon, bands like Wish for Eden, Focused, and The Crucified were signed to his label. Later, he would go on to sign bands like MxPx, Me Without You, and Underoath. But, early on, there were so many bands out there that Ebel wanted to introduce, he began putting out compilation albums. In June 1994, just a month before Cornerstone, *Helpless Amongst Friends* hit the stores. The fifteenth track on this sixteen-song compilation was our "Coming Back." People heard it, they liked it, and they came out to hear what P.O.D. was all about.

Between the compilation album and that set, our name was getting out. We began receiving contacts from folks asking us to play at their church or in their coffee shop. We took the ones we could do. And when we went back to Cornerstone in 1995, we had our own little tour booked on the way there. Normally, we wouldn't get paid from these gigs. Instead, it was, "Hey, we'll take up a love offering," or, "You can sell your merch." So, money was tight. But our expenses were just food and gas. We rarely needed a hotel because we'd just crash in someone's living room or we'd roll out sleeping bags in a church.

Up until this point, we all still worked full-time jobs. I can think of a lot of times we'd play a show in the San Diego area, then afterwards I'd rush to make it to my overnight gig at the grocery store. When the summer came, we'd take our three weeks' vacation and hit the road. But once '96 came and we started getting a name, we had a decision to make. Did we stay small, play local, and only tour during the summer? Or did we go all in with the band, trusting that this was a calling God was giving to us?

We went all in.

That doesn't mean that we didn't work. We just made sure that we had jobs that could adapt to our schedule. Wuv and I worked for his dad, my Uncle Noah, doing construction and landscaping. It was perfect, because the nature of that business meant that if we had to take off for a gig, we had the freedom to do so.

After my mom passed, I had moved in with some friends. At that time, I was still working the night crew. It was a good time. Every now and then it'd get a little crazy with everyone off doing their own thing, but we all got along. These were my homies from Maitland. We were already family.

Then my Grandpa Tom died. That was tough. He was a really good man. When he passed away, that left my Noni all alone. So, I moved in with her back on Maitland Avenue. She didn't need me to take care of her, but there was no way I was going to let her live alone now that both my grandfather and my mother were gone. I stayed living with my Noni until I married Shannon and moved into a tiny duplex in Chula Vista.

I FIRST MET SHANNON when I was around fourteen and she was twelve. My mom had remarried by that time, and I was living with my stepfamily. It was New Year's Eve, and we were all going to Disneyland. Each of us was able to take one friend. I took my homie, BJ, and my stepcousins brought this girl Shannon. It certainly wasn't a love-at-first-sight kind of connection. I mean, come on, I was only fourteen and I wasn't really looking for love, and certainly not with some twelve-year-old friend of my cousins. Instead, BJ and I were like, "Dude, we get to cruise Disney all night," and we took off.

I didn't see her again until a few years later. Another one of my Maitland homies, Ruben, was going out with one of Shannon's best friends. He was invited to Shannon's friend's birthday party, so of course he brought all of us with him. When I showed up, Shannon was there. Of course I remembered her, but in typical Sonny fashion, I pretty much kept to myself. When Shannon tells the story, she says I had my Walkman headphones on the whole time. While everyone else was mingling, I was sitting by myself listening to music.

More time passed, and by this time I was seventeen and she was fifteen. One of my stepcousins, the older sister of the ones who had invited Shannon to Disneyland, got married. The reception was at our house, and the backyard was packed. My cousins had invited Shannon to come along, and that's when I really noticed her for the first time. I wasn't totally sure about her at first. Our lives seemed very different. She went to a much nicer school—a white school. And in the neighborhood where I came from, she was only allowed to come so far before crossing into the "danger zone." But we hit it off, and we ended the night with a "Cool, I'll give you a call."

Our first date, believe it or not, was at the reception of her mom's second wedding. We had been talking on the phone, and I think I had visited her at her mom's house. But this was the first time it was like, "Yeah, we're on a date now." I bypassed the wedding and met her at the reception. We still laugh at the pictures. I'm at this fancy party wearing a big old Haile Selassie medallion. We're still the only couple I know whose first date was at a parent's wedding reception.

That first date was in the summer before my senior year. By fall—October 19, 1990, to be exact—I had asked her, "Want to be boyfriend and girlfriend?" She had come to visit me on my lunch break, and I knew I wanted to take that next step. Everything was great with us throughout my senior year and past my graduation.

Then came my first summer out of school. I had a little money in my pocket. I was partying with the homies. Basically, I was still a kid trying to figure out who I was. Part of that "figuring" was feeling out where Shannon fit into all of this. We started spending less intentional time together. But despite this, she was still always around. She and my mom were close, especially after the cancer diagnosis. So, even those times when we weren't technically dating, we were still tight friends.

But then my mom passed away and I asked God into my heart. It was at that point I realized that it was time for my transitional phase to end. But that was easier said than done. I was working full-time. I was doing the band thing. I was trying to be a good Christian while work-ing on figuring out what my purpose was in life. Pushing against the "I want to do good stuff" side were the facts that I was now twenty-one and living without rules with a bunch of my friends. Dude, my mind was all over the place. I had no idea where my heart was or where it even should have been at that time.

Then I moved in with my Noni, and I started spending a lot more time with Shannon. I was able to pull away from the craziness of living 24/7 with my homies. I real-ized that Shannon was my best friend and that I needed to stop treating her like she was just another person in my life. That's when I really started concentrating on our relationship.

A COUPLE YEARS PASSED, and me and the guys were on our way to Cornerstone '96. I was driving my uncle's Ford Explorer late at night, and all the homies were crashed out in the back. We were heading for a stop at my stepfather's house in Rosebud, Missouri, and I was cruising on some empty stretch of highway thinking about Shannon. I was talking and praying to God, trying to figure out what to do about our relationship. Wuv had already gotten married, and I was wondering if it was time I took that big step.

I was still young in my faith, trying to figure out how trusting in God worked. So, I prayed, "All right, God, if this is meant to be, give me a sign."

A shooting star flew across the sky. I almost swerved off the road.

Now, I know what you're probably thinking. *Dude, you're in the middle of nowhere, and there were probably a billion shooting stars going across the sky.* You're right! But I still had that childlike faith that was ready to see God everywhere. So I said, "No way, God. That was awesome. But I want to make sure it wasn't just coincidence. If it's really meant to be, can you show me another sign?"

Another star shot across the sky. I was like, "Dude, that's what's up!"

God has got so much patience with us. He could have said, "Man, I already sent you one star. Why wasn't that enough for you?" But He understood my simple faith, and He gave me what I needed. I long for the childlike belief I had back then. Now, after all these years, my faith in God is deeper and more well thought out. Unfortunately, that means that sometimes I find myself having to look much harder to see Him through all those layers of time and experience. It's like being at a concert and they turn on the smoke machines. All the details of what you could once see so clearly begin to get obscured. My smoke comes from my own so-called knowledge of who God is, along with the hurt and disappointment I've experienced over the years from people who call themselves Christians. I know that God is with me just as much as He was back then. His outline is just a bit fuzzier than it was when I was a spiritual newborn.

When everyone was finally awake, I told them what had happened with the shooting stars, and they were all freaking out. Somehow, out in the middle of nowhere, we found a pay phone. I called Shannon's dad and asked his permission to marry his daughter. He gave it, and it was all set.

Now, we started scheming on the best way to ask her. Shannon and a couple of my boys, Paco and Ruben, were flying out to Cornerstone to watch us play. We figured that would be the best time to do it. But it hit me that it had all come on so quick, I didn't even have a ring, nor could I afford one. As much as I wanted to give her something fancy, it would probably have to be some gumball machine ring instead with a promise of something better later.

We got to my stepdad's house in Missouri, where he and my two sisters were now living. I told him about proposing, and he was excited for me. He knew Shannon and loved her too. Me and the guys started talking again about how to do it and about the ring. My stepdad interrupted and said, "Hold on a sec." He left the room, and when he came back, he was holding the wedding ring that he had given to my mom. He said, "You don't have to use it, but it's yours now. Do whatever you want with it."

I have to admit, I got pretty emotional. I didn't even know he had it. After my mom died, my stepfather decided it was time to start over outside of California. He invited me to come along, but my life was in Southtown. So I said no. When he took off and my sisters went with him, there was really nothing left of my mom except maybe a few random trinkets here and there. When he gave me that ring, I felt like it was something valuable that was intimately connected to her. It was a piece of her that I was going to be able to pass on to Shannon.

So, now I had the ring, and by the time we left my stepdad's house, we had the plan. All that was left was to get to Cornerstone.

THE SET WAS GOING GREAT. The tent was out in a field. Inside, it was humid and it reeked. We were all sweaty and covered in dust from people moshing in the dirt in front of the stage. I was totally into the show, but I was also feeling some nerves because every time I would glance to the side of the stage, there was Shannon.

About halfway through, I stopped everything. I walked over and took her by the hand. I led her onto the stage, then got down on one knee and asked her to marry me. Despite my sweat and dirt and smell, she said yes. The crowd went wild. It was awesome. It was memorable. It fit perfectly for who we were at the time. And now, when I look back on it, I wish I had done it totally differently.

I don't know, man. I'm probably analyzing it way more than I should. But now when I look back, it just seems so forced. Instead of it being me and her, it was me, her, and a few thousand fans who probably hadn't showered for a few days because they were camping out at the festival. I did it for us, but I also did it as a testimony to the audience. It was my young Christian way of saying, "Look, everyone, this is the right way to do it!" Instead of thinking of how I could propose to make it perfect for Shannon, I had somehow involved everyone else and made it a teaching moment.

But even though I wish I had done it differently, I don't knock myself for it. We were kids. I had just turned twenty-three and she was only days from being twenty-one. I can't fault twenty-three-year-old, young, immature Christian me for acting like a twenty-three-year-old, young, immature Christian. Years later, once we were settled with a house and a couple of kids, I proposed again. It was Christmas morning. I had picked up a ring for her that was more her style, and I got back down on my knee. There was no one else there; no stage, no cameras, no muddy mosh pit. It was just me and this amazing woman who once again said yes to doing life with me.

WE GOT MARRIED ON NOVEMBER 2, about four months after the Cornerstone proposal. The ceremony was in an old-school kind of church on a lonely road. We had something like thirty people in the wedding party because I had all my buddies from Maitland Avenue and the neighborhood. Shannon had her friends and my sisters and cousins, along with some of the girlfriends of my old crew, in her party. It was a blast. All us guys wore Chucks with our tuxes. Theirs had black, fat laces, and I wore the fat white ones. Shannon looked incredible as she walked down that aisle. If I close my eyes, I can still see her like it was yesterday.

The golf course down the street had a banquet room, and we rented it out for the reception. We had no money for the party, but that was no problem. Luckily, some family members pitched in, and it was a great time. We celebrated into the night, then the next day Shannon and I took off on our drug-money-financed honeymoon cruise.

Yeah, I didn't see that coming either.

My Uncle Noah was running Rescue Records. When Rescue was getting off the ground, a family friend started helping support the business financially. He seemed to be a solid dude. He ran a trucking company and was very generous. It was no secret that Shannon and I had no money, so this guy offered to pay for our honeymoon. We were floored. We took him up on the offer and had an amazing time on our seven-day cruise to the Virgin Islands. The whole time we're thanking God for His amazing provision for us through this generous friend.

Sometime later, we learned that trucking wasn't this guy's only business. Dude, what the hell?

I'd seen this show play out before, and there was no other choice but to cut ties. We made sure he was out of anything even remotely connected with P.O.D. Eventually, he ended up getting busted and going to prison. He served his time, and he died not many years after getting out. Sad story. He was a family friend, and I had known him since I was a kid. I pray that he found his way.

Whenever I hear someone say, "The Lord works in mysterious ways," I think of this dude. I don't believe that this guy was ever part of God's plan for P.O.D., but I do know that whenever you try to love God and commit your life to Him, the devil will do everything in his power to try to mess you up. He will use whoever and whatever he can to throw you off the path God has set you on. Satan will even come in looking like a friend or a brother and try to destroy you from the inside. But God can take the crap the enemy throws at us and turn it into something good. Rescue Records went on to launch some great Christian punk and hardcore bands. Shannon and I are still in love and have three amazing kids who also love the Lord. And P.O.D. is still rocking over thirty years later.

A LITTLE LESS THAN A MONTH before I got married, P.O.D.'s second album, *Brown*, dropped. It was a huge step up from *Snuff the Punk*. We had more experience, better perspective on who we were, and a little bit more money to put toward the album. We had gone back to the same studio we were at before, but this time we recorded with someone who had more production experience under his belt. Once we had recorded everything, we went up to Hollywood to mix the record. We were there for a week, spending every day in the studio adjusting the levels and blending the tracks. Every night we crashed out together in the same hotel room, exhausted. If you listen to *Snuff the Punk* and *Brown* back-to-back, the upgrade in sound is very obvious. We still had our edge, but the low-budget rawness had been smoothed out.

We've been asked, "Why *Brown*? Is it San Diego brown? Is it Hispanic brown?" There were two reasons for *Brown*.

First, it's an acronym. You can hear me singing it on the song of the same name:

Believe, receive
Obtain, withstand
Never die

So, we've got that Christian message in there. But, honestly, the bigger reason is because it was just cool. It's kind of our culture. It felt right. And, most importantly, my aunt had that awesome brown pedal car that we wanted to put on the album cover. So, *Brown* it was.

Like the improvement in the production, the lyrics to the songs were also upgraded. In the time between the two albums, I realized that it was okay to get more personal. I could put myself into the story. So, instead of preaching to the audience, I began to try to relate to people. I was vulnerable. And no more so than in the song "Full Color."

The track begins with us behind the scenes riffing this funky groove. Everyone was doing their best to mimic their instruments, beatboxing, and just having fun. Then the lyrics start:

I cry why O' why did my mommy have to die?
Too many questions, no answers confuses my mind

I've got to think some people listening were like, "What the hell just happened? They were laughing and grooving, and suddenly he's singing about his mom dying." Today, when I look back on it, I wonder if I might do that all differently. But once again that's probably just me overthinking. Back then, there was so much freedom in what we did. Why put a fun, funky intro to a song where I'm pouring out my heart about the most traumatic event in my life? Why not? It sounded cool. Sometimes I long for the freedom of not overanalyzing my music.

"Full Color" was a link between me and my audience. It wasn't about who is right and who is wrong. It wasn't preachy or condemning. It was just me saying, "Dude, this is something real. This is what I went through. This is my pain. But this is what it took for me to open up my eyes and heart to Jesus so I could get some peace. Maybe He can do the same for you."

Brown was a very different feel from *Snuff*. But just because we weren't screaming "Abortion is murder" anymore, it didn't mean we didn't have a message and a purpose. And just like those vegan and straight edge and Krishna bands that we would find ourselves on a bill with, we were not going to back down from who we were. And unlike a lot of the Christian bands that we found ourselves playing with, we weren't part of the happy, joy, turn-the-other-cheek "Christian rock" scene. Our attitude was still, "If you say anything bad about our Jesus or mock our beliefs, we're going to throw down right here." That's the countercultural defiance you will still find in *Brown*.

When it comes to people accepting your music, I've found that counterculture is cool, as long as it's not about Jesus. When Bob Marley quoted the Bible in his songs, it was okay because he smoked herb and didn't talk about a Jesus-only salvation. When Santana sings about light and peace and love, it's all right because everyone's religious beliefs are acceptable as long as it's not Christianity. But because Jesus is like, "Salvation can only be one way," He is offensive. And anything offensive in our world is off-limits. Even though His package is love, grace, peace, and all that kind of stuff, it's still hate speech to a lot of people. That's because when you get down to the core of it, in order to receive that beautiful package He's offering, you have to change.

Don't get me wrong. That change isn't a prerequisite to getting right with God. Jesus isn't there with a ten-point checklist saying, "You've got to do this and this and this before I'll forgive you." All He's looking for is a heart that says, "I'm tired of doing it my way and I want to do it Your way instead." That's when forgiveness comes. That's when eternal life comes. And that's when the change starts. The change doesn't bring forgiveness; forgiveness brings the change. It's God's grace and true love that will make you a new person. You will change because you will be changed.

Living for Jesus is better than living without Him. That was our message, and we weren't going to back down from it no matter how much people might be offended by it. It's not that we were determined to be militant jerks. We were doing our best to learn how to communicate our message in a more effective way.

Still, the Bible makes it clear that if you follow Jesus, people are going to hate you. Why? Because they hated Him first. We were fine with people hating us because they hate Jesus. We just didn't want anyone hating Jesus because they hated us. So, rather than making our message angry, we made it cool. We made it edgy. We made it funky.

That was *Brown*.

6

WELCOME TO HOLLYWOOD

We were still playing anywhere that would have us. The only way we knew to make this band thing really happen was by working hard at it and touring as much as we could. Soon, word started spreading around about P.O.D., and it perked up the ears of some labels. Tooth & Nail Records probably would have been an easy get for us, but we didn't think that was the way to go. Brandon Ebel had done an amazing job with his label, but we weren't looking to stay in the Christian market. We felt our calling was outside the established church.

Some people didn't get why we were so determined not to go with a Christian house. Later, after we got our manager, bigger labels like Silvertone Records and others came knocking on our door. Jars of Clay had signed with Silvertone, and they had a big single on rock radio. That was huge news in the Christian world. People thought it was crazy that we'd give up Jars of Clay's label to go to some heathen, secular label. That's just Christian bubble mentality. Inside the church, there are a lot of people who think that anyone and anything outside the holy confines of the sacred believing community is evil. But our calling wasn't in the holy confines. It was to the bars and the clubs and anywhere else we could let people know through our music that there is hope in Jesus.

I'm not knocking any band who signed with Silvertone or Tooth & Nail, or even the big mainstream Christian labels like Word or Sparrow. More power to you! Do your thing! But I always felt like God was leading us down a different path, and we were pretty sure our road didn't end in the album racks of your local Christian bookstore. So, we toured and we prayed and we waited.

TIM COOK WAS A SEVENTEEN-YEAR-OLD former Californian living in the small town of Bartlesville, about forty-five minutes north of Tulsa. He was also a fan of Christian hardcore music, a genre that was lacking in rural Oklahoma. He decided to do something about it, converting a warehouse into a concert venue. After christening the new Where-House with a show by The Crucified, Tim hustled to make his stage a regular stop for bands who were passing through.

We loved playing the Where-House, and we loved Tim. Even though he was a short, white, business-looking dude, he was on our wavelength. He kept track of us as we grew as a band and told us, "Hey, if you ever need any help, just call." Eventually, that's just what we did. When touring and booking started getting to be more than we could handle, my Uncle Noah reached out to Tim and said, "Hey, my boys need someone."

Despite not having any experience, Tim took over as our official manager. The dude was great. He got us shows and he plugged us in to all kinds of Christian festivals. He was reaching out to labels and getting them to check us out. But there was still a problem. Tim kept his focus on the Christian world. It was great that he was keeping us plenty busy, and the Christian labels he was bringing in were cool. It would have been an honor to sign with any of them. But, again, was that the road we wanted to go down?

Tim finally started going after secular labels. At one point, we got some interest from Tommy Boy Records. They were putting out a lot of cool hip hop stuff that we loved, groups like House of Pain. Now, they wanted to move into the rock world. Jive Records started looking at us too. We were thinking, "This is so cool!"

We were weighing our options, still letting the labels come to us. But then Tim took a chance. He reached out to this Beverly Hills lawyer and convinced the guy to come check us out. I still don't know how the heck he pulled it off. We played a show in Hollywood, the dude liked us, and before we knew it, he started networking for the band. Suddenly, we're getting looks from everywhere. This lawyer was the one who first got us connected to John Rubeli.

Let me just say, John Rubeli is the man! He grew up as a Catholic kid who never really fit in. Maybe it was because he was listening to Depeche Mode and had hair like Robert Smith from The Cure. He was still young when he helped to start Lollapalooza, and soon he was booking all sorts of bands. He grew in the business and ended up as an A&R guy for Atlantic Records. The A&R person, or artists and repertoire, is like the middleman between a band and a label. They go out and discover acts, then report back to the label. Then once the label signs the act, the A&R dude is an advocate for the band to the label and the label to the band. It's a tough job when it's done right, and Rubeli knew how to do it right.

It was 1997 when he came to see us on tour at Walled Lake, Michigan. At that time, we were still touring with our old conversion van and a trailer. John came to our beater before the show, took a seat, and started giving us his spiel. We were trying to stay calm. This is freaking Atlantic Records! Tommy Boy and Jive Records were cool. But Atlantic is iconic. We're talking AC/DC, Led Zeppelin, Ray Charles—the list is huge.

We heard him out, then went in for the show. The venue was an all-ages type of club. It was basically a fun center with a stage. You pay your money to get in and you can either listen to the band or play Mortal Kombat and Street Fighter in the back. It was a Wednesday night, and we had about one thousand kids there.

John watched our show, then he took us out to Denny's after. That was a ritual for us before a long drive. We'd tell whoever was around, "Hey, we're going over to Denny's. Who wants to go?" Then we'd just hang out, eat pancakes or whatever, and talk with whoever was there.

So, we were there, and kids kept stopping by. John loved that. To him, that was what music was all about. He had gone from throwing these big shows to being an A&R guy behind a desk. Our show was giving him a flashback to an earlier time in his career. He was thinking, *These guys are the real deal. They just played a stage in the middle of nowhere, and now they're hanging out with their fans at Denny's, buying them food or just giving their own meals away.* John told us that he worked with platinum-selling artists who couldn't even pack out a bar. But we're nobodies and we've got one thousand kids coming out. He's like, "That's what music is supposed to do." He was sold.

JOHN GOT US A SHOWCASE at the Whisky a Go Go in West Hollywood. An Atlantic exec, Craig Kallman, was going to come and check us out. Kallman had recently done the *Space Jam Soundtrack*, which had hit double platinum and would eventually sell 6x platinum. In the US, you have to sell five hundred thousand albums to certify gold and a million to hit platinum.

We had a horrible show. The Whisky was always hit or miss because their sound system was a piece of crap. It's much better now that they upgraded it during COVID. But that didn't help us then. We met Kallman afterwards and it was all pleasantries and stuff. When we left, though, we were pretty sure Atlantic was dead in the water.

But later, Kallman hit John up and asked, "Are you sure about these guys? I'm giving you one shot to prove yourself. If you screw up, you're gone. Are you sure this is the band you want to take your shot with?" John replied, "This is the band I want to take my shot with." I've got to admit, it still chokes me up to this day that Rubeli risked it all for us. Kallman told him, "Okay, I'm going to let you do it."

Now, if you're thinking, "Sonny, dude, you should be grateful to Atlantic for giving you a shot," then you don't know the business. John was a small fish at Atlantic. If we didn't work out for Atlantic, they would chew John up and spit him out. We'd splatter on the pavement alongside him. Even after we hit it big and it all paid off for Atlantic, in my opinion they still treated John like crap. It pisses me off just to think about it.

John was the diamond in the rough that worked in an industry of monsters. All the big labels care about is money. Most A&R people will sign bands they don't even like, just because they think they might get them promoted to the next level. John only signed bands he loved; ones he believed in. He was one in a billion when it came to thinking that way in this industry.

That's all hindsight. At the time, we were still young and naïve. All we cared about was that a major label wanted us. We signed the contract, and we became Atlantic Records artists.

I don't know what I expected to happen when we were signing the papers. Maybe the heavens would open, the Holy Spirit would descend, and a voice would say, "This is my band. Listen to them." Instead, we took a few pictures, then drove from Hollywood back down to San Diego because we had to get up early the next day to work.

Wuv and I were still doing landscaping just to pay the bills. A few days after we signed, he and I were digging a huge trench, and we were up to our waists in dirt. The San Diego sun was blazing, and we were sweaty and dirty. I stopped for a breather. Leaning on my pick, I said to Wuv, "Hey, did you know that I'm a signed Atlantic recording artist?" Resting on his shovel, he nodded without smiling and replied, "Yes, I did. Did you know that I am also a signed Atlantic recording artist?" I said, "Yes, I did." We looked at each other a moment longer, then started back digging.

THE NEXT STEP was to find somebody to produce the album. We were on a budget, so we weren't sure who we could even afford. John used a demo to solicit producers, and our first hit was from a guy named Ed Stasium. He had done Living Colour's first few albums. We loved Living Colour because who wouldn't love a black rock and roll band? Stasium's portfolio was filled with other great bands too—The Ramones, Talking Heads, Motörhead. He was a great guy, and he was ready to work with us. In our mind, Ed was the dude for us.

Then we got a call from John Rubeli, and he said, "There's a guy named Howard Benson who digs our demos. I think we should take a meeting with him. He's a Pro Tools guy." We're like, "What's a Pro Tool?" John says, "It's the new thing. All computer."

That was all we needed to hear. No way were we going to let our music turn all computer sounding. Would Led Zeppelin record into a computer? Would AC/DC? Hell no! Forget it. Musical technology is just silly.

But John convinced us to meet with Howard. So, we went up to Hollywood and heard him out. He'd been around for a while but hadn't done a lot of big projects—maybe a few Motörhead albums and a Less Than Jake. Nothing gold or platinum yet. But we liked him. We dug the fact that he pulled up in an Isuzu SUV, not some fancy BMW or Mercedes. So, we're thinking he's pretty cool.

But there was still the stupid Pro Tools. Analog was what we were used to, and analog was where we wanted to stay. Hit record, do it in one take, hit stop. We told him, "Sorry, man, we're not going to plug into your computer and play. That's lame. We're not going to lose the big drum fill to some digitized percussion crap. We need to feel the music, feel the guitars." Howard said, "You're not going to lose that. You can still record to tape, but then I'll dump it into Pro Tools, and that will give me a whole lot of stuff that I can do with it."

Dude was totally right on. Once we saw what he did to *The Fundamental Elements of Southtown* with the Pro Tools, we were sold. By the time we recorded our next album, *Satellite*, there was zero analog. It was all digital. But for that first album with Howard, we were skeptical. Still, we signed with him, and we locked in studio time. For us, this was big time.

REMEMBER, we were just a bunch of kids from deep in SoCal. So, when the perks started coming, we were freaking out. First, each of us was handed a check for $5,000 and told to spend it on equipment. Traa had been working for a while before he joined P.O.D., so he already had a good bass set and a nice clean bass. He has pride in his equipment, and he always takes great care of it.

But with Marcos back then, his equipment was whatever he could afford at the time. He'd buy a rig, and it would last him until he needed to hawk it for rent money. There were times we'd even have to borrow equipment so he could play a show. But that's just who Marcos was, and we loved him. He was one of the family—you know, that younger brother who's always between jobs. There were times when he'd walk in with a bandage on his arm. We'd say, "You give blood again?" He'd reply, "Yup." Marcos is an artist, a musician—that's where his passion is. He isn't built for hard labor. Even today, I'll pick up his equipment for him and say, "I've got it, Princess."

When Marcos got his money, he bought a PRS guitar. It was his dream guitar because it was the brand Carlos Santana used. So, he got this great guitar, but then he bought a cheap Crate amp. John Rubeli walked in one day and saw his Crate equipment, and he was like, "Dude, what are you doing?" We joined in and clowned Marcos enough until he broke down and turned the Crate in, replacing it with a Mesa Boogie.

Next thing we got was a demo budget. It wasn't much, but it was enough for us to lay down a few songs. We knew an older guy from our church who gigged around town. He was turning his garage into a studio—nothing big, just padded walls and some equipment. We gave him our little budget, and we put together a demo. John Rubeli passed it on to Kallman, who must have thought it was okay. At least he didn't pull the contract. Those demos showed up again just a few years ago. We were looking for material to fill the expanded 2021 remaster of *Satellite* and decided to release those four songs on that album.

Beyond that, our perks included concerts and Lakers games and nights out. John Rubeli's love language is giving gifts. I can't tell you how many times he's surprised us throughout the time we've known him. One night right before we began to record *Satellite*, John pulled up in a rented limo. We piled in and he took us to see U2. We were floored. They were one of our top five bands of all time! At the concert, there were celebrities everywhere. Cameron Diaz and Christina Applegate were in the seats right in front of us. After the concert, Rubeli took us to an outdoor tent where we were told the band would be hanging out later. All throughout the venue were the "who's who" of Hollywood, making their rounds, hugging and kissing cheeks. We spotted Seal walking around the tent, and we had a chance to meet Fiona Apple.

The guy we loved seeing most was Martin Gore from Depeche Mode. The dude was legend. We were talking when suddenly Gore got down on one knee and kissed Marcos's hand. Guitar players are weird like that. If they think your playing is awesome, they'll give it up to you. It was a crazy night for a bunch of street kids from San Diego.

BEFORE WE STARTED THE RECORDING, Howard sent us to a rehearsal studio for two weeks. Studio time costs some serious money. Howard wanted to make sure we had practiced and were ready to record. He set us up at Mates in North Hollywood. There were three studios there, two small and one large. We posted up in one of the small ones and set to work.

It wasn't long before we discovered that next door to us in the other small studio was a band called Orange 9mm. We loved these guys. They came out of the New York scene and had the same kind of feel as Quicksand and Helmet, who we were big fans of. The lead singer was a black brother named Chaka Malik. Chaka was hardcore and New York through and through. We were blown away when we got to meet him.

That's the way it was when we were recording. Whether it was rehearsal or in the studio, we'd see people around us and be like, "You see who that is?" Once, when we were still at Mates, we were taking a break outside. We were just skating and hanging out, and a car pulled up. The door opened and this tall, skinny dude stepped out. We're like, "Holy crap, that's Marilyn Manson." The thing was that it was him, but it wasn't him.

At that time Marilyn Manson was the antichrist to the church, the Alice Cooper of his day. Christian leaders were preaching sermons about him and organizing pickets at his concerts. In their minds he was leading all our kids to hell. But that wasn't who we saw in front of us. Without his makeup and his goth clothing, he was just some ninety-pounds-soaking-wet dude who nobody would give a second look to.

Behind him, an MTV crew piled out because they were doing some story on him. He walked past us and said, "Hey guys." We're like, "'Sup?" That's when we started cluing in to the smoke and mirrors of the business. His marketers built him up like he's the devil himself, but it's all just a joke. It's a joke on the world. It's especially a joke on all the Christians who were afraid of their own shadows.

A while later, he came back out. He had his full look going on then. The MTV crew was still trailing him, and Brian Warner was once again Marilyn Manson. But we knew. We had seen behind the curtain. He wasn't the spawn of Satan. He was just a prank that Hollywood was playing on the world.

Our time in the rehearsal studio was huge. Not only did it prep us for recording, but it helped establish the feel of *The Fundamental Elements of Southtown*. Howard Benson, our producer, came and set up a recording system. Then, he just hung out and recorded us jamming. He was picking up all these sound bites because we had told him that we wanted the album to have a hip hop feel. That's why *Fundamental* launches with an intro and in between songs you hear drum bloops and jams and conversation. That was all intentional because we came from a hip hop world and we wanted to represent those roots.

FINALLY IT CAME TIME to record the album. They put us up in a two bedroom at the Oakwood Apartments, which were used by record, film, and television studios for temporary housing for artists of all kinds. It was crazy because we'd keep stumbling across actors and musicians just wandering around. We'd be hanging out by the pool meeting people, and they'd be telling us, "Oh, I'm recording too" or "I'm on set filming this TV show." And we're just like, "Wow, this is bananas."

Our recording studio turned out to be some guy's house. This dude was one of Michael Jackson's right-hand men, writing for him and recording him. He had a huge, three-story, fifteen-million-dollar mansion down in the valley. Howard Benson's engineer, a guy named Bobby Brooks, was living at the house at the time and convinced the owner to let him turn it into a makeshift recording studio. The third floor was the domain of the mystery man, and he never left it. The other two floors were where the recording took place. Behind one door was the control room, behind another was the drum room. Everything in its place spread throughout the house and basement.

The setup was still fairly new, and there hadn't been too many bands that had recorded there. Body Count had done some stuff, and Lemmy from Motörhead had recorded there. We loved it. The studio built in a house had just the jury-rigged, hip hop feel we were looking for. It being a fifteen-million-dollar home with a secretive Michael Jackson–connected guy upstairs just added to its mystique.

We began to record. Chris Lord-Alge had come on to mix some of the songs. We couldn't afford to have him on all the cuts, so we picked out the ones we thought he could bring the most to. This was the beginning of the Howard Benson, Chris Lord-Alge tandem. They blew up after the *Satellite* album, and soon everyone wanted the duo on their record. We really connected with Chris. I think we were his first experience with authentic Christianity. He saw that believing in God wasn't just about rules and looking down on people. There are people out there who can genuinely love God, love others, and be normal.

The same was true with Howard. He was a Jew from Philadelphia, and getting to know him on a deeper level beyond just music was one of the best things that happened during our recording sessions. Down the line, our relationship with him ended up connecting him with other Christian bands, like Flyleaf and Skillet. They'd be like, "Who did P.O.D.'s album?" Then they'd give him a call. To this day, because of all the bands that came to him based on our stuff, Howard still jokes, "Yeah, P.O.D.—they made me rich."

Recording is cool, but it's also a grind. We spent two months living at Oakwood while we put the album together. Still, we figured that's two months we weren't digging trenches out in the hot SoCal sun. When we recorded "Southtown," we knew it would be our first single. It had a hardcore, underground feel, and we figured it would get our name out there. But "Rock the Party" was going to be our more commercial hit. It was groovy, it was rappy, and there was a DJ in it. The song had the Beastie Boys feel we were going for, and it was just plain fun.

After we had been going at it awhile, Howard came to me and said, "I'm going to send you to the throat doctor." I'm like, "Dude, I've been screaming my guts out for years now. I've never seen a doctor. Why start now?" But he convinced me, so I went.

Suddenly, I found myself at some fancy Hollywood medical office. At one point, the doctor covered my nostril and said, "Breathe in." I did. Then he covered the other and again told me to breathe. I couldn't. What the hell? He said, "You've got a deviated septum. You're only breathing out of one side of your nose." When did that happen? And how didn't I know? The doc told me it could have come from wrestling around or getting punched in the face. Or it's possible it happened just from rubbing my nose too hard. That last option sounded seriously lame, so I went with the punch.

I needed to get it fixed, but there was no way I could deal with it then. It's not like we were going to stop recording so I could have nose surgery. Besides, I'd been doing okay with it until then. So, I put it off, and I kept putting it off. My schedule was just too insane. It wasn't until sometime after *Satellite* came out that I finally got it fixed.

The other thing Howard set me up with were vocal lessons. To me, that was like the ultimate rock star treatment. Once or twice a week, I'd pull up to this Hollywood multimillion-dollar house in our broken-down touring van. I'd ring the doorbell, and Ron Anderson, my vocal coach, would let me in. Ron was the quintessential "vocal coach to the stars." He worked with everyone from Axl Rose to Neil Diamond to Tom Cruise. But don't go thinking that he was some kind of diva. A gentleman through and through, he would pause the lesson of whomever he was with just so he could personally answer the door and show you to his living room. He was an amazing man, and I was very sad to learn that he passed away in 2021.

Once, while I was waiting, I was listening to this chick do her warm-ups. Her voice was very distinct. I started freaking out that it could possibly be who I thought it was. I was a huge fan of her movies like *Kalifornia* and *Natural Born Killers*. Sure enough, when she was done with her lesson, Juliette Lewis came walking out and gave me a wave before she left. Dude, what life am I living right now?

Eventually, we finished laying everything down for the album. Now came the waiting game. Nothing in the music industry moves quickly, and it was going to be a while before *Fundamental* dropped. So, we did what we always did; we hit the road.

7

THE WARRIORS COME OUT TO PLAY

The Warriors.

Every band has to have its fans. That's just logic. No fans, no one is buying your music. No one's coming to your shows. But it's not enough just to have fans. For a band to really make it, it's got to have superfans, its rabid fans, the ones who follow every move you make and make it to every show within a six-hour drive. You see them at every concert because they've pushed their way to the stage. They're singing every lyric because they know the songs even better than you do. Every day they're repping your gear at school, while they pass out to everyone who will take one a bootleg copy they burned of your cassette.

For P.O.D., these were the Warriors. They were our hardcore base. For them, we weren't just the music they listened to. We became part of their lives; we were their identity. They connected with us because so many of these teens and young adults had spent most of their lives living like we did—in between worlds. They had grown up stigmatized by the world of religious traditionalism. There was a certain way that many of them were expected to look and act. When it came to music, there was a line that they were forbidden to cross.

Every generation finds the standards of their parents constricting. Many adapt and take on the culture of the past. But there are others for whom those expectations wear like a straitjacket. It wasn't that they were lacking love for God, but they wanted to express that passion in their own way. Their comfort zone was in torn shirts, leather jackets, and Doc Martens boots. They were pierced and tatted and mohawked. Their joy came in the pit, their worship in hardcore. When you looked at the crowd pressed against the front of the stage, you couldn't pick these Warriors out from anyone else. It's only when you talked with them that you might find that some of these searchers were a bit further along in moving beyond their pasts and finding some hope for their future.

Most churches took one look at these punks and said, "Not a chance. Not in this holy sanctuary." A lot of them were asked to leave youth groups because the parents were afraid they'd rub off and suddenly little Jimmy would start doing drugs or sweet, innocent Susie would find herself knocked up. Too Christian for the hardcore and too hardcore for the church. Sounds a little familiar.

When they first heard P.O.D., they discovered a band that was speaking their language. They'd slip on their headphones, turn on the *Brown* album, and hear someone yelling at them:

> Look at my soul, what do you see?
> Imagine a moment, You don't know me.
> Who am I, I am you
> Who am I, I am you.

They're like, "Damn, this dude gets me." They'd keep listening, and two songs later, they'd hear the same voice quoting from the Old Testament prophet Joel about visions, then singing, "Jesus Christ is what I see." A band that could talk about God from a real-life perspective while laying down a jam they could play at full volume from their car speakers and not be embarrassed. Suddenly, these alternative Christian youths had a home. And, like magnets looking for metal, they began to find each other. Sometimes it was at concerts, sometimes on message boards, sometimes it was another dude wearing a P.O.D. shirt in your English Comp class at the community college.

Eventually, this groundswell of P.O.D.-ites took on an identity. They became the Warriors. They were the core of our fan family and, in a very practical way, were the reason we eventually hit platinum.

Many of these Warriors have stayed with us through the years. I can remember playing a gig after P.O.D. went big. We were at a club in New York, maybe the Irvine. The Rollins Band and Three Doors Down were on the bill with us. It was mainly a secular crowd, but as I looked in the mass of people, I saw faces I recognized. Old Warriors who had been with us forever. There was a cool bond whenever we locked eyes. It's like I'm saying, "I see you," and they're like, "Yeah, Sonny, I'm still here." Then the music would start and they're in the middle of it. They're destroying the pit. They're dominating. They're in there doing what they came to do. The only way to recognize them from anyone else was that they were the ones who, when they accidentally laid someone out, would pick them back up.

I knew they were there for the music, but there was more to it. They were there to be a light in a dark world. Not only had they picked up our music, they had adopted our mission.

At some point, being part of the Warriors took on a visual element. I remember looking at the line before the shows and seeing Warriors wearing face paint. People would be eyeballing them like, "Dude, what's with the war paint?" But they had a secret, and when the time came, they'd show everyone who were the real old-school P.O.D. fans.

Once the concert would begin, I'd see our Warriors out in the crowd. I'd pick some dude out, and during a song, I'd jump on a barricade in front of him. He'd bust out the paint, and when I got back on the stage, I'd be sporting the Warrior paint. Everyone would be looking around like, "What the hell just happened? Why didn't I know about this? Hurry, someone paint my face!" Meanwhile, all the Warriors would be feeling their O.G. vibe, like, "Yeah, Warriors . . . that's where it's at."

I can remember when we told our tribe about signing to Atlantic Records. We were at Cornerstone, and nobody knew yet. We played the show, then said, "Hey, we've got some exciting news. We've signed to Atlantic."

Everybody went nuts. This kind of thing just didn't happen. Stryper had signed with Enigma back in the early eighties, and MxPx was with A&M. But this was freaking Atlantic Records. For our Warriors, it was like this was their justification. This was their affirmation that, "Yeah, we picked the right team. We went all in with these guys, and we nailed it."

It was truly a symbiotic relationship. They helped us get popular, and when we did go big, they felt the victory. They dug it when they could find their fresh P.O.D. shirt at Hot Topic and wear it to their high school. They'd be like, "Yeah, that's my band. They've always been my band. You're not taking that from me." It was a cool feeling for them and for us. For all the love they sent our way, we had the same kind of love for them. Remember, we're just street kids from Southtown. We'd lived in a constant state of "What the hell are we doing here?" We had a lot more in common with the fans coming to our shows than we did with all the rich industry people who were working behind the scenes.

AFTER WE FINISHED cutting *Fundamental*, we went back to touring. It was good knowing we had the record coming out, but in the meantime we still had to grind. Atlantic threw us a little bit of a tour budget, so we traded in the van for an old bus and hit the road. Project 86 joined us in our new transport, while Blindside followed along in their van.

It was a good tour, but when we got back, we decided to make a shift in the way we did things. I've already mentioned a bunch of bands that we toured with, and there were plenty more like NIV, Dogwood, and others. What was similar about them all was that they were Christian bands. That meant that we kept playing to a lot of the same crowds in a lot of the same venues. We needed to branch out. When we went back out the next time, we took with us a metal band called Guano Apes, fronted by Sandra Nasić. They were blowing up in their home country of Germany and were trying to transition into the States.

Not long after, we jumped into another tour with The Urge. They had just signed with Interscope, and we dug their sound. They were fronted by a brother named Steve Ewing, and they brought a cool reggae and ska influence to their music. When they took us out, we started playing clubs and hitting the college scene. It opened the doors to a whole different side of the music scene from playing Christian festivals or Christian-based clubs.

It was about this time that John Rubeli came up with another of his great ideas. We wanted to keep momentum up while we waited for *Fundamental* to come out. He suggested we go back to Brandon Ebel to see if he would be open to releasing an EP (a shorter-version album usually under thirty minutes long) on Tooth & Nail. Brandon was killing it with his label, and he was down to drop something for us.

We put together a few demos of tracks from *Fundamental*, along with some other songs like "Full Color" and a cool, acoustic guitar piece by Marcos called "Rosa Linda." When it came time to name the EP, we didn't struggle too much. This was a thank-you to our fans for being there when we were grinding just to get by, for putting us up in their guest rooms and on their living room floors, for feeding us and supporting us and driving five hours just to sweat in some church's basement that we had overloaded way beyond the fire code.

What better name than *The Warriors EP*?

FINALLY, IT WAS TIME for "Southtown" to release. It was our first single from *The Fundamental Elements of South-town*, and it got some decent play on college radio, but it wasn't huge. Atlantic still wasn't really buying into us, so we weren't getting any push from them. Any opportunities we got came from our own inner circle—us, Tim Cook, John Rubeli, we were doing it all ourselves. We were hustling and, like always, doing whatever it took to push this record.

Les Claypool from Primus was always keeping an eye out for up-and-coming bands. He heard "Southtown" and was like, "I dig these guys." So, he invited us to join his band on tour. We freaked out. Primus is one of the baddest bands around, and we were touring with them. It was another of those "What is going on here?" moments.

This was back in 2000, when MTV still showed music videos. Starting in the early eighties, MTV began to completely change the music industry. No longer was it enough to just record your music. You had to have a killer video with it. If *Fundamental* was going to really hit, we needed some kick-ass videos. We started with "Southtown." We knew we didn't want a crazy, abstract work of art. We're a live band. We wanted the audience in front of us. We wanted people to see us play and the crowd reacting. This was our Southtown anthem. Forget the FX and CGI. This had to be real.

At that time, Marcos Siega was still an up-and-comer in the video business. Since then, he's done a ton of music videos, directed a bunch of TV shows, and even done a few movies. We told him what we wanted, and he nailed it. For Wuv and me, nothing was more Southtown than Maitland Avenue because it's where we started. So, Siega set up a stage in front of the houses we grew up in. We invited all our homies and the neighbors, and we blasted the song. When you watch that video, those aren't actors. We didn't ship anybody in from Hollywood central casting. That's our life on that screen. It doesn't get any more real than that.

The video made a lot of noise, not just among fans but among other bands. They loved seeing the crowd reacting to the music. Artists started contacting Siega and telling him, "We want a video like P.O.D." Soon, it became a subgenre. Siega kept the same feel with "Chop Suey" for System of a Down and "Last Resort" for Papa Roach. You can't watch either without getting "Southtown" vibes.

You've got to stop and realize how big this was. Forever it had been Christian groups copying secular bands. Christian bookstores even put out charts with lists just to help parents keep their innocent teens from the devil's music. "If you like Rage against the Machine, you'll like P.O.D. If you like Refused, you'll like Blindside." Christian music was in the role of playing catch-up. And most of what came out of Christian mainstream music sucked like the cheap knockoffs that they were.

At some point in history there was a cultural shift. Originally, if you wanted to find the greatest composers and artists in the world, the most imaginative painters, the most brilliant minds, you would find them in the church. The pioneers of everything creative and beautiful expressed their brilliance out of a love for God or out of their struggle with God. But somewhere along the line, the church got so caught up in its puritanical fears of not breaking any moral laws that it ran away from art. If it's not overtly tied to something from the Bible, then it can't be worshipful. And if it's not worshipful, then it is obviously of the devil. The church chased out the creative risk-takers. These were the ones who worshipped God by expressing through art His creative beauty found in nature. They praised Him through music that let you clap on two and four instead of one and three.

Humanity was made to appreciate beauty. When the church abdicated its creative role, the secular world filled the vacuum. And it did a pretty good job with it for a while. But, as always, when there are no moral limits, people will chase the extremes, and that is where we find the art world today. So, when the church cries out about pornography and death metal, it needs to ask, "How much is our responsibility? How much of a role did we play by relinquishing our lead role in the arts?"

Sorry, didn't mean to chase that squirrel.

What I started to say is with the "Southtown" video, suddenly the secular world began to take notice of "Christian music." P.O.D. was developing a reputation in the industry as a band that was cutting-edge, both in its creativity and in what it stood for. That's all we ever wanted, to be respected for our music. We were a band that had a mission, not missionaries who had formed a band. Our reputation as a group you wanted to listen to made its way out to the listening public. P.O.D. was getting noticed. Then that whole *TRL* thing happened.

TOTAL REQUEST LIVE, known as *TRL* to those who watched, was a daily show on MTV that would count down the top ten videos of the day. Who chose the videos? The viewers. Every weekday when the phones would open, music fans—teens and young adults mostly—would call in and vote for their favorite video. The highest vote-getters made the show, which was a huge deal. A massive audience would get exposed to your music. If you hit top ten, you were pretty much assured some serious record sales. You hit number one and the sky's the limit.

P.O.D. was perfectly set up for the *TRL* algorithm. Why? We had the Warriors. Our fanbase was determined that we were going to make the show. They knew that if we did, it would not only let the world know who P.O.D. was, but it would legitimize them as fans. When "Southtown" came out, the Warriors jumped into action. There was a certain window, convenient pretty much only to the East Coast, when the phones would be open. But our fans didn't care about convenience. They burned up their speed dials. "My vote is for P.O.D. 'Southtown'!" Thousands of calls poured in, and they got us onto the show. We started to get nationwide notice for the first time.

Marcos, Traa, Wuv, and I were freaking out. These punks from the barrios south of San Diego were suddenly being talked about in a TV studio in the heart of New York City. And when they played the video, the world learned who P.O.D. was. "Southtown" only made it to seven or eight on the list, but that was enough. Our sales skyrocketed.

We were already shooting the video at that time for "Rock the Party." John Rubeli pulled us aside one day and let us know that *The Fundamental Elements of Southtown* was on a trajectory for a gold record. That was crazy to us. Not long after, we paused the video shoot and presented Howard Benson with his first gold record. It was our first too, obviously. But for Howard, who had been in the music business so much longer than us, to finally get a gold was a major milestone. Of course, since then he's gotten enough gold records that he could melt them all down and overlay his house. But this was the first to go on his wall. So, we made it this big thing. And by "we," I mean John Rubeli. He was always ahead of all that. Nothing made him happier than making other people happy. Honoring Howard was just another example of John being John.

When we made it onto *TRL*, it forced MTV to say, "Who are these guys?" At that time, *TRL* was mostly all pop. Typically, it was a battle between Britney Spears, Backstreet Boys, NSYNC, and Hanson for the top slots. Korn and Limp Bizkit had hit with "Freak on a Leash" and "Nookie," but they also were big-name bands at the time. The execs at MTV looked at us like, "What's a P.O.D. and how did they get in here?" But MTV understands trends, and we were trending. We rolled out spring 2000 on the MTV "The Return of the Rock Tour" with Staind, Dope, and Crazy Town, and they included us on their *MTV The Return of the Rock* compilation album.

Once we got our foot in the door, we knew we had to kick it in the rest of the way. That's why we went with "Rock the Party" as our next single. That was going to be our crossover song. "Southtown" was too heavy to hit number one. But "Rock the Party" had that Beastie Boys vibe that appealed across the market. You listen to it, you just have to dance. We brought Marcos Siega back and told him we wanted the crowd vibe again. But this time, instead of focusing on our SoCal roots, we wanted to show the diversity of the band and of our audience.

What does Siega do? He piles us all in a bus, puts in a runway, and sets us loose. First thing you notice is the makeup of the band. You got a black dude on bass, a Latino on guitar, a Filipino on drums, and a dreadlocked lead singer with a seriously long 23andMe rap sheet. But the diversity was in the crowd too. In the bus you see people from every kind of background dancing and having a good time. There's the mohawk guy and the cholo and the surfer dude with the sweet goatee. Along the way, we pick up teens from a basketball court and some tatted chicks hanging out on the steps. There are piercings and bandanas and multicolored hair, and everyone is having a blast. Then, when the bus finally pulls in, there's a stage already set up. We're playing and the crowd is totally into it. In the background, we've got this sacred-heart-of-Jesus-looking mural, and a Chinese dragon is weaving through the crowd. By the way, if you look closely, you'll see that mural Jesus appears to be sporting some serious dreads of His own.

Somehow, Siega managed to get everyone and everything in there, including all our families. That was our whole point, and really it is our whole goal as a band. The bus was pulling over and picking up people of every culture, every race, and every religion. We were out to grab human beings from all over the world because we were about to rock the party. And it worked. It was a perfect blend between music and mission. We made our purpose clear right from the beginning. "We came here to rock this jam, spread His love is His master plan." We were intentional in our aim, but we were also finding ways to be universal in our appeal.

ONCE WE WENT GOLD, Atlantic Records decided we were finally worthy of their attention. Between them and our team, we landed a spot on Ozzfest 2000. We're talking main stage Ozzfest, not a side one. Sure, we were one of the opening acts, but we weren't complaining. We were just freaking out seeing our names on the same poster as Ozzy Osbourne, Pantera, and White Zombie. I mean, come on, man! Behind the scenes, we blended into the daily grind of rock and roll life. The Osbourne kids were still young, and we got to know them and Sharon pretty well. This would come into play a couple years later.

"Rock the Party" was released while we were on tour. Our Warriors once again kicked in and got us into the top ten. But this time all those pop kids whose votes normally went to Britney and the boy bands were like, "Hey, I like this song!" They threw their votes our way, and on July 26, 2000, we hit number one. Suddenly, MTV was coming to Ozzfest to film us. Our name was everywhere. We're getting played all over the US. We're hearing from new fans in Europe. And we're just standing there with our mouths hanging open, watching it all happen.

MTV called and said, "Hey, we want you guys in studio." Yeah, that'll cause a double take. We were so humbled and excited when we arrived. Carson Daly was there and started asking us questions. But no one had really prepared us for what we were supposed to say. Instead of talking about our album or Ozzfest, we start bumping up all our friends. "Dude, you guys need to check out Incubus. Deftones latest? Come on, man, that's where it's at." We didn't go in with a plan to talk about other bands. We just didn't know what we were doing. But we did learn about the power of the voice that we suddenly had. It wasn't long before Incubus and the Deftones entered the top ten. You say something on the biggest platform in music at the time, people are going to listen.

LOOKING BACK, I can see now how God used those Warriors to build our platform. We were hugely grateful for all that was happening, and we were confident that God was in control of it all. Word got around quickly that we were a Christian band, but our music was good enough that fans listened anyway. Over time the message started sinking in for some. I don't know how many times I've had people say, "Sonny, when 'Set Your Eyes on Zion' would come up, I'd always smoke a big, old bowl. But then, about ten years after I first heard it, I was getting ready to light up and I was like, 'Wait a minute. He's talking about God.

What's that about?'" Then they'd tell me how they started reading their Bible and going to church. Soon they were changing their ways and getting right with God. Man, you don't know how that makes me feel.

And so often it does take ten or fifteen years for the message to hit. Most of the time it wasn't people saying, "The guys have a message and I better pay attention to it." It was rarely that obvious. Typically, they discovered the band first, and only later did they realize there was also a message. It took time for the truth to soak in. I've got to remind myself of that a lot. All those years of going in and playing bars, I'd finish up, wondering if anyone heard anything. I'd find myself asking, "God, did you do anything? Did we just waste our time and Your time?" Making music is not my purpose in life. It is the medium for me to accomplish my purpose, which is to let people know that life with Jesus Christ is better than life without Him.

For me, the impatient frustration began to build. I wanted to see God part the Red Sea right before my eyes, but it wasn't happening. But then we started hearing stories like the Zion one above. Or, another time, when a guy came up and asked, "Hey, you remember when you played Dreamstreet in Ocean Beach?"

"Yeah," I answered. "That place doesn't even exist anymore."

Dude's eyes started leaking, and he said, "Well, you played there on a Tuesday night, and I was in the back. It was the worst time of my life. But something you said stayed with me. I ended up getting remarried, and I got saved."

By that time, he wasn't the only one with tears. I said, "Man, thank you for sharing that story. You don't know how many times I've asked God, 'What are you doing with all these nights?'"

I've learned I've got to stop asking God so many damn questions. All they do is prove my lack of faith in what He's doing. If He's called me to this life of being out on the road and missing my family, I've got to quit doubting and just do my job. And I've also got to stop and look at what He's done in the past. If I ever have any doubt whether God is in P.O.D.'s journey, I only need to think back to what He did with our next album, *Satellite*, and all my hesitations will disappear.

HERE COME THE BOYS
FROM THE SOUTH

The band was back in San Diego. The recording sessions for *Satellite* were starting soon, and we still had a lot to get ready for. Step one—it would be good if we had some songs. Okay, that's a bit of an exaggeration. We had songs. We just didn't have *the* song. It was getting tense.

John Rubeli had warned us. He said, "Okay, you've just had this crazy success with *Fundamental*. Platinum record. Now's when the real stress comes. Now you've got to figure out who you're going to be." We loved Rubeli. He was like a big brother who was concerned about us because he'd seen it before. Bands get some success, they start thinking they're something special, then they implode because suddenly everyone's a rock star.

Truth be told, we had some of that happening already. Howard Benson had come down to our practice sessions to check out what we had so far, which wasn't much. Tensions were pretty high, especially between Marcos and Wuv, because everything was kind of sucking at the time. Eventually, it just blew. Wuv jumped up from his drum set and shoved Marcos. Marcos went flying backwards, sacrificing his body while holding up his guitar, because he knew which would be more expensive to fix. Once he was back on his feet, though, Marcos apparently forgot the price tag for his guitar. He cocked it back and was ready to take Wuv's head off. Traa and I jumped in to stop him. Meanwhile, Howard, who isn't a confrontational guy, was watching us and probably thinking, *Let these idiots beat each other up. I'm not getting into that.*

A quick P.O.D. fun fact: When you listen to "Boom," you hear Marcos launch the song with a sweet riff. Wuv builds it with the snare, then suddenly, I jump in with "Pusher!" which came out sounding more like "Pushah!" I would like to think that in my thirty-plus years with P.O.D. I've written some beautiful and thought-provoking lyrics. But it seems the one I get asked about way more than is remotely necessary is what that one stupid word is at the beginning of "Boom." That push fight had become a running joke in the band, and for some reason the word just burst out of me. Now you know, so quit asking.

One of those days at the rehearsal studio in San Diego, we were trying to write, but it wasn't coming. Howard said, "Let's walk to the 7-Eleven, grab some coffee." We trek down, grab our drinks, and we suddenly hear all these sirens. Then, police cars and firefighters and ambulances started flying down the street. Above us, helicopters were following the first responders.

This was before smartphones, so we rushed back to the studio and turned on the news. That's when we saw them talking about Santana High School in Santee just down the block from us. A student had taken a gun to school and began shooting kids. This was just two years after Columbine, and teens shooting up their schools was a lot rarer than it sadly is today. We watched the whole morning as they took the kid into custody, then counted the casualties. Two teens killed. Eleven more wounded, along with a couple school supervisors. It was tragic.

Not long after the shooting at Columbine High School in Colorado, we were out touring. This was 1999. Somehow, someone got hold of us and asked us to play at a healing kind of service at a church in Denver. We rerouted so we could play the show. A bunch of the Columbine kids went to this church, and we had a powerful time just letting them all know that they were loved.

At the rehearsal studio, we were reeling. Between that day's shooting and our connection to Columbine, our day of rehearsal wasn't going to happen. We just sat there, each in our own thoughts. Marcos was fiddling with his guitar and said, "Man, we need to write a song about the kids. You know, about the youth." No doubt—we were all on board. The word *youth* resonated with us because it had kind of a punk and a reggae feel to it. Marcos nailed it down even more when he said, "Yeah, this song needs to be about the youth of the nation." Soon after, he came up with that opening riff—very somber, a lot of feeling and mood. It perfectly fit the sorrow and helplessness we were feeling over that morning's shooting at Santana High.

133

THAT'S HOW IT'S ALWAYS BEEN for the band. The hand of God shows up when we aren't expecting it. We started the day with the goal of getting through a rehearsal without one of us beating someone else's ass, and we finished it with the main structure of what many consider to be our best song ever. I can't tell you how many stories I've heard from teens and adults who heard "Youth of the Nation," and it pulled them back from suicide or gave them hope in the middle of a terrible time in their lives. We always live with that attitude of, "Okay, God, we're ready whenever You are."

Same type of thing happened after we had begun recording *Satellite*. The label had once again put us up at the Oakwood Apartments. We'd record through the week, then go home for the weekend while Howard took all we had laid down and worked his "Boogie Woogie" Benson magic on it. One Friday back at home, I wasn't feeling relaxed at all. The guys had laid down a track for a new song that we had been working on. It was a feel-good song like "Boom," but it was more than just a fun song. But it wasn't dark or brooding like "Youth" either. This song had some power to it and a great vibe. Now, all it needed were some words. No pressure.

Unfortunately, I had nothing. This song hung over me all weekend. On Monday, everyone was counting on me to come back with some killer lyrics. When Sunday night arrived, it was time for Shannon and me to head back to Hollywood. I asked her to drive, hoping I could come up with something at the eleventh hour. My daughter, Nevaeh, wasn't even a year old yet. She was in her car seat in back, and I'm watching her in the headlights of the passing cars because it was better than staring at a blank notepad. People had always told me, "Your daughter looks just like you." But I hadn't seen it.

At least not until that moment.

I cried out, "Oh my gosh!"

Shannon freaked out. "What's wrong?"

"Dude! She looks just like me! I can totally see it!"

It was the most incredible feeling. This beautiful, tiny person was a part of me. There was no denying it. I grabbed my pad and wrote in the glow of the map light, "Every day is a new day. I'm thankful for every breath I take." It just started flowing. God took over. I wasn't even hearing the melody now. I was just writing my heart. I got to the chorus with my daughter's perfect little face in my mind.

"I, I feel so alive, for the very first time. I can't deny you."

How could I ever deny God and the perfection of His creation after seeing me in my daughter and my daughter in me? We are not just random acts of evolution. We aren't just disposable, interchangeable cogs in some naturalistic wheel. We are intentional masterpieces of a Creator God.

Call it divine inspiration; call it a creative infusion. None of the guys was surprised the next day when I pulled my pad out of my backpack and told them I had the song. Again, that's just the way God always seems to work with us. Howard and I pulled away to hone the song. I had cleaned it up from its first pass in a semidark car driving northbound on the 101. Typically, on my pads you find words all over the place, along with phone numbers and doodles. And my handwriting when I'm in that creative mode, it's not really messy, but it's also not ready for prime time. So, by the time I would bring Howard in, I'd have made it a lot more legible so that he could follow along as I sang.

One addition Howard made to "Alive" was the last line of the chorus: "And I think I can fly." If you're wondering what "I think I can fly" means, I must admit to you that I have no idea. Howard added it. He said it sounded cool. He said it was easy to sing and it felt good. I told him, "Dude, it's cheesy and it sounds like a Disney lyric." Ultimately, he won out. And he was right. It's a great lyric for that song despite it making absolutely no sense.

Normally, Howard's help was less with the words themselves and more about how I should sing them. He'd weigh in telling me I should pronounce certain vowels a specific way or I should emphasize this word over that. He was also on me all the time making sure I didn't drop the ends of my words and that I enunciated them clearly. All those things I learned from him back then, I still use today.

These days when I write, I don't use notebooks or pads as much. Now, as I'm going through the day and something hits me, I type it into the Notes app on my phone. A lot of times they're just one-liners that I'll go back later and re-visit, sometimes on my own and sometimes with the guys. Like with our latest album, *Veritas*, I was like, "Hey, let me read you some of these titles and thoughts. Let me know if any of them sticks." If they dug any of them, I'd put a check by it to go back again. That's the way my creative process has always been. A moment of inspiration, then fleshing it out later. I was never one of those "Oh, I think I'll write a sad song about young love today" kind of guys.

In fact, 95 percent of the time when we're recording, the band is hearing the lyrics for the first time. We'd talk melodies and other things. I'd tell them, "This is kind of what I'm hearing," but then they'd trust me with the rest. Experience told them I'd come through. It was that way with "Youth of the Nation." They'd done a lot of the guitar and drums and bass, at least roughed in. The fills and ambient would come later. It was my turn, so I went in to show Howard what I had.

I started, "Last day of the rest of my life." That was all it took for him—he was sold. Howard's a lyric guy. He later told me, "Dude, that is one of the most powerful intro lines I've ever heard. In eight words you've already painted the story." We worked through the rest, then took it out to the guys. They listened and were like, "This is good, man." Initially, our chant was heavy on the "We are, we are," but it was Wuv's idea to give it more of a melodic, reggae feel with an emphasis on the final syllable—na-TION. We began building the song in the studio, bringing in the tympani and eventually the kids' choir.

Having the kids come in was a trip. Our first idea was to put out a call to our fans in LA. Any locals could come in and we'd record them on the chorus. Gene Solomon, our old lawyer, stepped in and put the kibosh on that. He said it had the potential to be a liability nightmare. Who knew? So, we went to Plan B. In Hollywood you can find anything. We tracked down a kids' choir and brought them in. On recording day, we set up a bunch of food and snacks. We wanted to make it an event for our special guests. The kids showed up, and Gene made sure all the parents who came with them signed the waivers. We mic'd them up, and they started singing.

As soon as you hear the kids come in, it's both exciting and eerie. It's one of those chills moments. These were the youth I was singing about. They brought a feeling of innocence to a very dark song.

FROM THE JUMP we knew "Youth" was special. It was the same with "Alive." As far as mood, the two songs were polar opposites. But we knew both would draw listeners in. Both songs had messages to them, but we don't want to be a preachy band. We intentionally work so that we don't come across that way. That's why *Satellite* opened with "Set It Off" just to set the mood. Next came "Alive." But between that song and "Youth of the Nation," we sandwiched in "Boom" as kind of a kick-ass palate cleanser. In fact, you'll find on the album plenty of songs written purely to rock, ones like "Masterpiece Conspiracy" and "Portrait."

Over time, we had gotten to know some cool artists in the industry. That led to sweet collaborations. "Without Jah, Nothin'" featured H.R. from Bad Brains, which was huge. He is the O.G. of blending hardcore punk and reggae. Legendary Jamaican Eek-a-Mouse gave us an amazing collab on "Ridiculous." We brought Christian Lindskog from Blindside onto the song "Anything Right." Blindside was a Swedish band that wasn't getting the play they should have because they were pigeonholed into that "Christian rock" category. We hoped that seeing Christian's name on our song list would turn some people on to Blindside's music.

As we put the album together, we were always aware of ensuring that the Gospel message or some level of God-talk was in our music. Like I said, we're not preachy. But we always found ways to get the truth in. We had to. It's who we are. It's what the band is all about. We found ways to do it that wouldn't cause people to say about us, "Hey, here's a Christian band that's actually pretty good." We wanted them to be like, "P.O.D.'s new album is amazing!" Then, as they're listening, they'd start thinking, "Check it out. I think they're talking about God here. I guess that's cool."

My attitude going into songwriting is, "God, You're going to say whatever You want to say. And I'll trust You to say it the right way." Because of that, most people will listen to our music and think, "That's a great melody and a cool lyric." The God part of the songs to them is like the teacher in Charlie Brown, "Wah, wah-wah-wah-wah wah." But in God's timing and His intention, there will be a point for some when they'll say, "Dude, he's singing about God. And what he's saying makes a hell of a lot of sense." I can't tell you how many times over the years I've had someone tell me, "Sonny, remember when you sang this?" or "Remember when you said this at your concert? Dude, it was just exactly what I needed to hear." Often, I'm thinking, *I don't think I ever said that, and I know that's not in any of our songs.* But that's because it wasn't me talking to them; it was God.

WHEN THE RECORDING was in the can, it was time to figure out how to roll it out. There was a push from the head of

Atlantic's radio department to launch with "Boom" as our first single. We knew the song was going to be big. It was our ESPN song—still is today. Every time it's played at a Padres game or a NASCAR race or as an MMA walkout song, I'll get texts, "Sonny, I heard 'Boom' again!" It was fun, and it had that Southtown vibe. When people hear it, they know the boys are back at it.

But as we sat with Howard and talked it through, we decided to come right out and hit them with "Alive." We knew that song was *the* song of the album. Why not launch as strong as we could? The song released July 31, 2001. Less than six weeks later, a bunch of psychos flew planes into the World Trade Center, the Pentagon, and a field in Pennsylvania.

Before I get to why "Alive" was the perfect song for 9/11, let me explain why "Boom" was not. Actually, I probably don't need to explain it, because it's pretty obvious. Not long ago, I read this article about how Clear Channel, which owned more than 1,100 radio stations, sent out a memo right after 9/11 with a list of 164 songs they were going to temporarily ban from their playlists. Some of them make sense, like Tom Petty's "Free Fallin'," Savage Garden's "Crash and Burn," and Drowning Pool's "Bodies" that contained the chant "Let the bodies hit the floor." Other songs, you've got to kind of wonder about, like "Ob-La-Di, Ob-La-Da" by The Beatles and "Peace Train" by Cat Stevens, which seem to be the exact kind of songs you should want on the air.

It's no surprise that Clear Channel blacklisted "Boom." If we had gone with the label's recommendation, our release would have hit a full stop. But instead of having the exact wrong song out, we had the exact right song. Call it luck, call it coincidence. I call it God's hand once again reaching in and making it all work. When 9/11 hit, "Alive" was already number one on *TRL*. Suddenly, everyone was desperate for hope. Everyone had a conscience. We were united as a nation of survivors. Across the country, families and communities came together, put their arms around each other, and sang at the top of their lungs, "I, I feel so alive for the very first time, and I think I can fly!" It was perfect. It was beautiful. It was the song that many in America needed, and God chose us to give it to them.

AFTER THE TERRORIST ATTACK, *TRL* shut down. MTV shut down. New York shut down. It was that way for a time, while everyone tried to get their feet back under them. Slowly, life began to come back online. Less than two weeks after it went dark, *TRL* was ready to start back up. But how do you do that? *TRL* was the biggest show among young people at the time. What do you say to the millions of kids who were looking for answers and for hope?

Turns out that was a question I had to face head-on. I got a call from MTV saying they wanted me on for the first show back. No one was really flying yet, so it was going to be a phone interview. I think it was me, Lenny Kravitz, and Enrique Iglesias, who had a beautiful ballad out called "Hero" that was also perfect for the times. I can't even remember much of what I said. I just tried to remind people that there is hope in the world.

Not long after, *TRL* flew Wuv and me out to New York City to be on the show. It was bizarre. Just six days before 9/11, we had performed live on *TRL* from Battery Park less than half a mile from the World Trade Center. When we went back, everything was different. They took us as close as they could to Ground Zero. There was still ash everywhere. Here and there were unclaimed parked cars piled high with ash, and the guys showing us around told us the cars probably belonged to people who had died in the buildings. But amidst all the somberness, as we walked, I heard plates clinking and people loudly talking to each other. Looking toward the noise, I saw a restaurant that was open and people who were just trying to find their way back to normal. It was an eerie contrast.

When we got to the show, my buddy Johnny joined us for the interview. He was a San Diego firefighter who was there crawling through the rubble, helping out where he could. Dude, it was rough being there. We didn't know what to say. But, once again, I felt God taking over. I told the viewers that we can't know why these things happen. But we do know that God does. He loves us and He's bigger than this kind of evil.

It wasn't preachy. I wasn't throwing Scripture around. It was just an opportunity to remind people, "Dude, God loves us, and He loves New York." My focus wasn't on what happened on September 11. I wanted to point to September 12 and beyond. That's what was inspiring. All that mattered to us was that we were Americans. What mattered were the heroes, like Johnny, who were digging in the rubble. It was the New Yorkers loving on the first responders and passing out water to them—that was America. That was all of us.

IN THE WEEKS AND MONTHS TO COME, we started doing more shows. That was just what we did. We have always been a touring band. We knew that on stage is how we earned our fans. They may have seen P.O.D. on a flyer or a poster and wondered who this band with the initials was. When they saw us play, they knew. So, from the beginning we were out on the road. Again, initially, it was with other Christian bands, but then we started pairing up with other very non-Christian bands.

Sometimes we had to make tough choices when it came to touring. Back in 2000, we were invited to go on the road across the US with Korn. It was a huge break. Korn was the big dog. But when I checked out the timing, I had to call the guys in the band and tell them I couldn't do it. My first daughter was due during the tour dates. There was no way I could be gone for that. Marcos, Traa, and Wuv were bummed but understood. But then Korn came back and said, "Well, we're going to Europe in the summer. We'd like you to come then." Uh, yes please!

We kept on the road because that was where we were making our money. We weren't getting paid yet for the albums. That would come later when we'd negotiate a new contract with Atlantic. The road was paying our bills and building our résumé so that we could go to our label and say, "Hey, look, we're selling albums, we're packing out shows, we're blowing up MTV. It's time you dropped a serious contract on us." We were out with Primus and Sevendust and any other band who would gig with us. At one point, we even took an up-and-coming band called Linkin Park on the road with us.

Back to late 2001. We were on David Letterman for the first time. It was just a couple days after Christmas, and his only guest was former New York Mayor Rudy Giuliani. Letterman liked to keep the studio cold, and I mean freezing cold. I was seriously worried my voice was going to crack. Turns out that's exactly what it did. We did "Youth of the Nation," which had released exactly a month prior. The Brooklyn Youth Chorus backed us up, and they laid it down!

Four months later, we were back in New York City for *Saturday Night Live*. That was big time. We had done Leno for *Fundamental*, and Letterman was cool. But we had grown up watching *SNL*, and now we were the musical guest. We got there early and watched the cast practicing their skits. This was the era of Will Ferrell, Tina Fey, Amy Poehler, and Jimmy Fallon. Alec Baldwin was hosting. We had to keep asking ourselves what we were doing there.

While we were hanging out backstage, this dude suddenly bounds into the room. I said to myself, "That's Stephen Baldwin!" He was seriously high energy, but he was totally cool. He pulled me aside and said, "You guys are the Christians, right?" That led to a good talk before he suddenly took off again. When I heard later that he had become a Christian, I was so happy for the guy. It was a reminder to me that I can never write anyone off. I've got to take every chance that God gives me to show love to the folks He puts in my path. You never know what He's going to do in their lives down the road.

At that time, we were meeting all kinds of people. You'd have these brief encounters after the show or in our down time. And it was never, "Dude, can I share something with you?" Instead, I believed that God could use anyone's smile or a simple word of encouragement. You never know what God is doing. His hand is everywhere working if we open ourselves to being used by Him.

Jumping ahead, in 2012 when I went back on the road, I took my son, Justice, with me. He was kindergarten age at the time. I'll talk about it more when the time comes, but on that tour I felt the least amount of pressure I ever had about my mission as a Christian in the rock world. In fact, I hardly thought about it at all. My only job was to protect my son. I was there to watch over his heart and his mind and to be a daddy. And a teacher. Before we left, Shannon loaded me up with his coloring packs and his homeschool books and said, "Make sure you're doing this every day with your son." It was awesome, and I loved it.

It turned out being a daddy was the biggest witness I had ever had in P.O.D. Bands and their crews were coming up to Justice and me in catering and saying, "Hey, dude, I'm watching you and your son these last two months. It's been beautiful to see." A lot of guys out on the road, they're there to get away from family for a while. To them it's a free pass to step out of their marriage and let it rip. I wasn't there to guilt them into anything. I wasn't there to preach to them. I was just there to try to live the way I believe a husband and father should. It wasn't long before I started seeing more kids and more families showing up on tours.

God doesn't always call us to "do." Sometimes He just wants us to "be." I do rock and roll. I do my mission. But I am a father, a husband, and a believer in Jesus. It's those last three that will truly make a lasting impact on this world.

9

THE BALLOON BURSTS

Fame changes everything.

I'm not complaining. I'm not saying it's good or bad. And I'm also not trying to make it sound like suddenly P.O.D. was a household name. We weren't Aerosmith. We weren't the Rolling Stones. Even today, I'm guessing that half the people who see our name show up on their playlist for the first time ask, "Who the hell is Pod?"

But our name was getting out. The vast *TRL* mob knew who we were. The big arenas knew who we were. We were getting recognized. That could be really cool at times. It could also go to your head.

I'm amazed at bands that have been around for decades and still have their original members. Like U2—they have that much talent and such big personalities and it's still just Larry, Adam, Bono, and The Edge. Radiohead and Coldplay both got their starts near the same time P.O.D.

did, and they're sporting the same roster. But the list of bands with their original lineups is short for a reason. Being together on the road twenty-four hours a day takes a toll. Learning how to respectfully create together is a challenge. And keeping your head on straight when everyone is telling you just how awesome you are? Dude, that is an almost impossible task.

When fame came to Marcos, Traa, Wuv, and me, it was like overfilling an old tire. As the pressure of popularity increased, our cracks and weaknesses started stretching us until finally we blew.

WE WERE STILL THE DARLINGS OF _TRL_. When the end of 2001 came around, MTV invited us to do their big New Year's Eve Party. It had only been three-and-a-half months since 9/11, so the million or so people who usually show up in Times Square were told to stay home that year. A lot of them didn't listen. They gathered on the street below us while we played indoors. As always, it was a wild time. The highlight of the night was when Ja Rule joined us just after midnight for Bob Marley's "Get Up, Stand Up." It was epic.

We barely had enough time to go home and tell our families we loved them before we took off across the ocean. Initially, the label didn't push _Satellite_ internationally. They still didn't believe we had that kind of play. It had been the same with _Fundamental_. To them, we were an American band with an American sound and American fans. We made it to Europe back then only because Korn took us. But now that Atlantic saw that we had some serious momentum, they got in gear and sent us overseas.

"Youth of the Nation" was releasing here in the States about the time we reached the other side of the ocean. It was a whirlwind. They sent us all over, hitting MTV in Italy, doing pressers in Germany. It wasn't anything like touring—just media all day long. We'd show up in a country, and there would be record execs and media people waiting to meet us. We'd smile for pictures, answer some questions, wave to the fans, then take off for the next city.

Japan was next on our itinerary after Europe. That was wild. Japanese fans can be flat-out nuts. Even though we were just there on a public relations trip, we ended up playing a show, because apparently that's just how things are done there. How all these non-English-speaking fans could sing along with our music still amazes me. Smiles, interviews, waves, then back on the plane.

Next stops were Australia and New Zealand. That was just plain fun. We ended up playing a number of quick shows—kind of one-off punk rock types of things. In one New Zealand radio station, we pushed everything against the walls in one of their rooms, set up, and played a set. That's rock and roll.

When we finally got back home, we weren't going to let the grass grow under us. We jumped right back into touring the States again. Then, in May, we went back overseas, headlining our first tour in Europe. We were on top of the world. We had done what we set out to do. We were one of a handful of rock bands that actually made it to the top. Our résumé was strong. We had all the juice we needed to go into Atlantic and tell them to pull out their checkbooks. It was finally time we got seriously paid.

IMAGINE GOING TO CITY AFTER CITY, then country after country. Everywhere you go, people are telling you how awesome you are. You are the best musicians, the best songwriters, the best performers. "The lyrics of your songs changed my life." "I've never seen a live band lay it down like you guys." Fame is beautiful, man, but she's a liar. She'll sweet-talk you, tell you that you're somebody special. You aren't that street kid from Southtown anymore. You've left that life and those people behind. You are Sonny Freakin' Sandoval! Yeah, fame is beautiful. But when she's done having her way with you, she'll chew you up and spit you out.

Dude, I love my wife. Shannon made sure that I never thought more highly of myself than I should. There's nothing nasty or snarky in me saying that. Shannon is real life. The road is not real. MTV is not real. International press telling you that you are a superstar is not real. My wife handing me my precious daughter and saying, "Baby, your little girl loves you, and right now she needs a diaper change"—that is real. And it is beautiful. Shannon, along with my faith and my upbringing, are what kept me sane. I am and will always be that street kid from Southtown.

Traa had a family. Wuv had a family. Their wives and kids did for them what mine did for me. Being from a broken home, I always wanted to be a dad and have a family of my own. It's like a boat sitting out in a bay. If its anchor is firmly set in the sea bottom, it's safe. If there is no anchor, there's no telling where it will drift. My family keeps me moored to solid ground.

I've wrestled with this next part of the book. Marcos Curiel is like a brother to me. We have been through so much. He is an artist and an incredibly passionate man. There was a long period when I would have told you that what happened to P.O.D. was all Marcos's fault. I was pissed beyond measure with him and wanted nothing to do with him.

But time goes by. Passions cool. Age brings wisdom and opens ears to both sides of the story. As I tell what comes next, I'm doing it from the point of view I had at the time. If at any point it sounds like I'm pouring all the blame on Marcos, keep reading. Eventually, it will come back around to the place we are now, loving each other, creating together, living life as brothers in this musical family.

AGAIN, WE ARE NOT a Christian rock band. I'm not knocking the genre, despite how it sometimes sounds. There are some great Christian bands out there. But despite our roots in church basements and Christian clubs, our calling was not to stay there. Our heart was to take God's truth out to the world, not to remind Christians of the truth they already knew.

There were many in the record industry who, as soon as they heard us mention God, automatically downgraded us to a subcategory. "They're not a real rock band. They're a Christian rock band." To them, all Christian bands were B-listers, at best. Even today, there are those in the music industry who will never take P.O.D. seriously because, in their minds, Christian rock inherently has just enough suck in it to not make it worth their while.

What's interesting is that I think there are a lot of believers in Jesus who feel the same way about Christian rock. "Yeah, we love our bands, but we know they are only B-listers. If only we could get one of our bands on the A-list." So, when P.O.D. really hit, a lot of those church rockers made sure that everyone in their circle knew that those dudes who do "Boom," they're Christians.

Dude, I even fall into this sometimes. When Flyleaf first joined us on tour, I was very protective of them. Here was a bunch of Christian kids who had an amazing sound. I remember thinking, *I don't want people viewing them as just another Christian band. People need to know that Lacey and her band are killing it.* I think back to that now and I realize my own bias. I automatically put the Christian rock genre into second tier.

None of us liked to be dumped into that category, but for Wuv, Traa, and me it was something we just learned to live with. If someone came up to one of us at a show and said, "Dude, you're my favorite Christian band," we wouldn't say, "Man, what are you talking about! We're not a Christian band." But if someone said that to Marcos, he'd make sure they knew what was up. He was sick of hearing P.O.D. called Christian rap rockers or a Christian nu metal band or whatever other qualified subgenre someone came up with.

Around this same time, the years of being together so much for so long started wearing on us. Just like a constant drip will eventually wear through cement, all the little things between us began turning into big things. This was especially true for Marcos. He was a little more lackadaisical when it came to working a "j-o-b." He was usually short with his end of the rent for the practice studio and was always perfectly comfortable letting someone else pay for his carne asada burrito after practice. But we were all cool with it because it was Marcos. We were family, and that's how family rolls.

After the success of *Fundamental Elements*, and then seeing *Satellite* take off like it did, there wasn't quite the same need to take care of our little brother anymore. And, honestly, I know that Marcos never wanted to be in that little brother position, but that was just how our different roles played out. Many of the running jokes and jabs that accompanied being the "little brother" began to sound in his ears like disrespect. He was the lead guitarist of a platinum-selling rock band, dammit. You don't talk to him that way.

The thing was, he wasn't wrong. I know my attitude toward him was changing. My respect for him was taking a hit. I was getting tired of what I perceived to be a growing diva attitude in him. That led me to say and do some stupid things that only made the situation worse.

One of the worst incidents was when we were on the press tour in New Zealand. They took us on this cool safari tour that was about an hour-and-a-half away from our hotel. We were all just hanging out around the facility when Marcos said, "Hey, I want to go back to the hotel." We're like, "Dude, kick it with us. The driver isn't going to drive you and your wife ninety minutes to the hotel, then drive back here to pick us up. Use your common sense." But he was determined to go. That was when I said something to him that was very mean and very personal. It drove a wedge between us, as I knew it would the second it left my lips. Years later, Marcos let me know just how much what I said had hurt him, and I apologized. He was gracious enough to forgive me.

But the pressure in the band kept building.

AFTER OUR EUROPEAN TOUR we got asked to play Ozzfest again. This was when the money really started rolling in. We had gotten to know Sharon Osbourne back when we first played the festival in 2000, and for some reason she took to us. We were like young kids that she saw something good in. So, when Tim Cook was negotiating for 2002, she was like, "I'll give you what you want." We ended up signing for $65,000 a show for thirty shows.

We didn't know what to do with money like that. We weren't even a headline band. There was one thing, though, that we knew we wanted to get with our new pay grade. Before you knew it, we were touring with three buses and a semi. Wuv and I were on one bus with our families. Traa and Marcos were on the second with our tour manager, Dan Hallas, and NYC Smitty, our security guy. And our crew rode in style on the third bus.

It was a crazy season, and when we came home, we turned right around and launched the Youth of the Nation tour. We were on the road that whole year nonstop. When we finally got home, we were exhausted. It was time to get a little rest while Tim Cook began the negotiations with Atlantic for our payday.

WE WERE HOME FOR THE HOLIDAYS. Stress-free downtime after so many months on the road. I couldn't wait to spend time with Shannon. Wake up with my daughter climbing on me. Check in with the homeboys. Christmas at Noni's with the family all around couldn't come quickly enough.

Then I got a call from Tim, our manager. "We've got to meet," he said.

So, Traa, Wuv, and I got together with Tim, and he said, "Hey, I don't want to blow this up or get all crazy or anything. But Marcos has started another band."

We blew up.

Fundamental was platinum. *Satellite* was on trajectory to go triple platinum. We had worked our asses off on the road for the last three years with our eyes set on one point—that day when Atlantic was finally going to pay us what we were worth. This was that day! Now was that time! The label had already come to us with a crazy high number, but we had pushed back. "You can do better," Tim Cook had told them. And they did! They countered with an even more outrageous number, but still we held off. We knew that we were stacked to push them even higher.

Then Marcos started his side band. That may not sound like that big of a deal, but to a record company it plants a seed of doubt. "Sounds like there's some dissension in P.O.D. Are they going to stay together? Is Marcos's heart still in it?" This pet band of his had the potential to send our whole payday crashing to the ground.

This wasn't the first time Marcos had sabotaged us. One show on our last tour, he had begun to purposely play the wrong parts during our set. Afterwards, we all went face-to-face.

"What the heck, dude?"

He admitted that he had done it on purpose. His excuse was that we were all jaded. We weren't in it for the music anymore, he said, we were just going through the motions. "It's always you three against me," he complained.

Well, now that he started his second band, he was right. It was us three against him, and we were finally ready to get what was owed to us. We had sacrificed time with our families so that we could support them. Every time we came home from the road, our kids had changed. Marcos didn't understand that sacrifice. He didn't have kids yet. He brought his wife with him on the road. Dude was sabotaging our payday, and we were not okay with that.

WE STILL HAD A CHANCE TO FIX THIS—one more try before it all got shot to hell. It was Super Bowl XXXVII, and the Oakland Raiders were playing the Tampa Bay Bucs at Qualcomm Stadium in San Diego. There were events the whole week, and we got slotted into one of the many parties. Tim Cook was doing his "keeping the peace" thing and arranged for us all to meet in the dressing room after the show and talk it all out.

We played our set, but when we came back to the dressing room, there were people all around. I mean, it's the Super Bowl. How we thought we could get some quiet time alone, I don't know. But, quite honestly, I don't think a quiet place would have mattered. When the opportunity to talk was in front of us, I don't know that any of us really tried. Instead, we just did our usual stuff, then left. My friend Guido who was hanging outside said that when I walked out, he could see the sadness on my face.

Communication has always been one of our biggest downfalls as a band. I don't know if it's because we're all men or if we just all suck at talking about feelings. What I do know is that we lost a huge chance to maybe make things right. I don't know if that's what would have happened. But what is undoubtedly true is that if instead of just being pissed off at Marcos, I had said, "Dude, you're my bro. We're in this together. Let's talk about this," then we might have at least had a possibility of reconciling the issue.

I didn't say anything. Marcos didn't say anything. Neither Wuv nor Traa said anything. Marcos left the dressing room, and he left the band. At least from the perspective of Wuv, Traa, and me. Marcos will tell you that we all mutually agreed on his departure. Whatever. The result was still the same. Our perfect résumé for the label just blew up. Instead of a four-man band rocketing to the top, we were a nu metal trio without a guitarist. Try selling that to Atlantic.

NO ONE KNEW MARCOS WAS GONE. How long could we keep this hidden, we wondered? Long enough to get a contract signed? People always say that it's not the crime, it's the cover-up. We knew that hiding Marcos's departure from Atlantic would be wrong. So, the question was not if but when.

That decision was made for us. We were approached to do a soundtrack song for the movie *The Matrix Reloaded*.

On top of that, we were told that we would be the lead single, which meant shooting a video.

Crap.

There's a story in the Old Testament about Shadrach, Meshach, and Abednego. The king issued a decree that said whenever people heard this certain music, they needed to bow down and worship a giant statue he had made. These three guys said, "Sorry, king. We'll only worship the true God." The king got so mad he had them thrown into a fiery furnace. But when he looked inside, the king couldn't believe what he saw. "Didn't we throw three guys in there?" he asked. "I see four of them, and one of them looks like a son of the gods!" The king had the door opened, and the three original guys came out not even smelling like smoke.

I could just see the execs at Atlantic watching the Matrix video. They'd be digging the music until one of them said, "Didn't we sign four guys to a contract? I only see three." Rather than coming out of the fire, we'd get tossed in. And rightfully so.

But before we said anything, we wanted to record the song. We obviously needed some guitar help, so we flew in an old friend from Little Rock, Arkansas, named Jason Truby. He had cut his teeth in a Christian metal band called Living Sacrifice and was an incredible musician. A true technician. He came in and did an amazing job with that soundtrack song, "Sleeping Awake."

Tim Cook went back to Atlantic and told them about Marcos. He had our Matrix song with him, hoping that it would soften the blow a bit. You know, "Sure, Marcos is gone, but P.O.D. is still strong. Listen to this."

Yeah, that didn't work.

When Tim told them, they were like, "Okay, cool. Don't sweat it." But when they came back with their counteroffer, it was way below what they had proposed before. We were floored. So much work. So much sacrifice. So damn close.

But that's when our Southtown roots kicked in. Instead of us fighting back and making a big deal out of it, we went back to our underdog mentality. We took it as a challenge. So we got gut-punched—what else is new? The Man has been trying to keep us down our whole lives. Screw him. We'll just go back and do what we did the last two records. We'll go in and work our butts off some more. We'll make a great record, and we'll prove to the label that we're still P.O.D. even without Marcos.

It didn't hurt that we had just gotten that payday from Ozzfest. Sure, Atlantic was going to shell out far less than we knew we deserved, but each of us still had enough to keep our families housed and fed. So, it was back to business as usual. Well, almost. We were still short a guitarist.

Jason had done an incredible job with "Sleeping Awake." We figured he'd be perfect to fill Marcos's place. True, he was a virtuoso Arkansas white boy who'd be trying to fit into an ethnic rap reggae rock band from south San Diego. But he loved God. He was a hard worker. And he could play fire. So, he jumped into the band, and we pushed forward.

10

COVERS AND CHASMS

I love that there's been a resurgence of record stores. So many hours of my teen years were spent at Tower Records flipping through the stacks. Cover after cover would drop onto the one in front as I dug for something new, something cool, something I hadn't seen before. When I'd find something, maybe Suicidal Tendencies' *Join the Army*, Sade's *Diamond Life*, or Public Enemy's *Yo! Bumrush the Show*, I'd take it up front, pay for it, then carry it out in one of those square yellow bags.

Once home, I'd peel off the clear plastic, slip out the sleeve, then let the vinyl disc slide onto my hand. After spooling it onto my turntable, I'd set it spinning, drop the needle, then sit back and feel the music. You've got to leave the liner notes for the second listen. The first time through is all about the experience.

At least that's how I imagine it would have been if I could have afforded vinyl records or a record player. Sadly, vinyl was a little too fancy for me. So, I contented myself with cassettes, usually copied from a friend. Of course, there were those rare times when I was lucky enough to have the original. Then I could be the guy making the copies. It was that duping tapes philosophy that helped us when P.O.D. was just starting out. We couldn't afford to give away CDs. Cassettes were the currency of the underground music scene. "Here's our tape. Copy it all you want. Give it to your friends."

Eventually, the music industry shifted from analog to digital. Vinyl and cassette followed the path of the dinosaurs, while CDs became the industry standard. The record labels were flying high. It was ridiculously cheap to mass-produce and distribute CDs. And, because it was new technology with higher-quality recordings, the record companies jacked up the price. When CDs first came out, you could get new music for $12.99. But then the prices started going up. Pretty soon, it would cost you $18.99 and sometimes up to $22.99 for an A-lister's new release. Considering it probably cost around 75 cents to make it, it's no wonder the record companies were swimming in money.

Then in 1999 some teenager in Massachusetts created a peer-to-peer file-sharing program called Napster. People started sharing music online. The record labels cried "Piracy!" Music listeners responded, "Screw you!" The labels got the courts to shut down Napster. The listeners shouted out, "Screw you even more!" The record companies were in the fight of their life, because Napster had launched a new medium for music, and there was no going back. Why should consumers pay $18.99 for a CD, when all they were going to do was load it onto their computer and eventually onto their iPod Shuffle? They wanted the labels to give them a way to skip all that transferring business and have the music come directly to their computer. It would be so much easier. And so much cheaper.

Suddenly, the record labels were left wondering how they were going to make up all that lost profit. Their conclusion: they couldn't. Panic set in. Record companies began mass layoffs. Whole departments were fired. Artists were abandoned. Label employees who survived the initial axe went into work each morning wondering if that day would be their last. It was as if a giant chasm had opened in the recording world and people and acts were being swallowed alive. It was onto the edge of this cliff that our next album, *Payable on Death*, was balanced. When it finally tipped in, it was not because anyone pushed it. Instead, it was simply that there was no one left at Atlantic who cared enough to keep it from falling.

MARCOS WAS OUT and Jason was in. It sucks that it happened the way it did, but as I look back now, I see that the break had to take place. It was necessary for the growth of the band and for my relationship with Marcos. I'm not saying that I'm happy that everything went down the way it did. It's just that as I look at the place where Marcos and I are now after more than thirty years of friendship, I can see that it was all part of the overall plan. We are now more like brothers than we ever were.

At the time, though, him leaving took me into some dark places. I had tried so hard to be the good guy despite all the rock and roll temptations that you'd expect and that seemed to be around every corner. It's 100 percent true—the greater the success, the larger the trap. We had hit the top of the charts. We were bona fide rock stars. We had the life that most dream of, and it was getting harder and harder to say no to all the perks that came with being a celebrity. Out of love and loyalty for God, I tried the best that I could. I didn't want to become the "sex, drugs, and rock & roll" stereotype.

I believe that all the guys felt this way. But this was just so new to us, and it sometimes felt that at every turn God was leaving me hanging. There seemed to be no quid pro quo in the relationship. Shouldn't I be getting some sort of special blessing for trying to do the right thing? Instead, I get Marcos leaving the band and a crap contract with Atlantic.

It was this frustration with God that got me so excited about having Truby join the band. He seemed to have his head on right. Straitlaced. Sober. Not jaded like the rest of us. Having him around could bring some much-needed spiritual refreshment. Jason joined us and we went to the studio to record *Payable on Death*. We were optimistic coming off the incredible success of *Satellite* and the Matrix song. Our Warriors couldn't wait to hear what we would put out next.

We went with Howard Benson again to produce. We knew him; he knew us. Wuv, Traa, and I rented a house in the Hollywood Hills. Jason moved his wife and newly adopted daughter into the Oakwoods. Living in two different locations didn't help with the initial blend. Becoming this new version of P.O.D. was going to be a learning process. Marcos and Jason are two very different players. Marcos is self-taught, soulful, with a Latin vibe. Truby is a student, mathematical, more complex. We'd tell him, "Dude, just lay back on that part a bit." Laughing, he'd say, "I can't." It was an adjustment for all of us.

Jason had an additional challenge. Like I mentioned before, he was a fish out of water when it came to San Diego. It would have been hard enough for anyone to suddenly jump from obscurity into a multiplatinum rock band. But he's got the whole culture thing to deal with. It's like a small-town kid watching *Boyz in the Hood* for the first time or sliding an N.W.A. disc into their player. They'd be like, "What is this?" It's a whole different world.

Eventually, we developed a groove and started cranking out some great music. I loved "Will You" right from the beginning. It's one of those great, feel-good songs with some real meaning behind it. But "Change the World"—we figured that would be our great, uplifting anthem from the album. It had the potential to be our next "Alive." The video that accompanied the song was incredible. The director used the entire budget to travel the world and shoot real people holding signs with lyrics from the song. If you haven't seen it yet, you need to put down the book and open up YouTube.

We dropped a lot of great music onto that record. And if the album wasn't already epic enough, Phil Keaggy came in and played on a couple of the tracks.

PAYABLE ON DEATH was a great album. We fully expected it to follow the path of *Satellite*. But then everything began to go stupid.

It started with our album cover. The Christian bookstores hated it. This wasn't the first time we had to deal with this idiocy. As I mentioned earlier, our original cover for *Snuff the Punk* featured an angel holding a gun to the head of the devil. That was deemed far too dark—we wouldn't want to promote firearm violence against the prince of darkness—and the poor angel was relegated to fighting Satan with only his fists.

When *The Fundamental Elements of Southtown* was released, on the cover was an amazing piece of art by pop-surrealist artist Jean Bastarache. It's full of symbolism, and I think it is easily the best of all our covers. But the Christian retailers had a fit. "It looks pagan," they cried. "Is that a Hindu meditating?" Worst of all—and I have to admit, we went way over the line here—there was a cigar depicted in the artwork. Just imagine, if Christian bookstores stocked that album, it wouldn't be long before all the boys from youth group would be storming the 7-Eleven to buy up the entire stock of White Owls and Swisher Sweets.

But business is business. The fledgling religious arm of Atlantic couldn't lose the Christian market, so they created an alternative cover with a thick black frame that covered most of the offending symbols. The rest of the label's divisions thought it was as silly as we did, but at least Christianity was saved.

Now, let me just say that I know these bookstore execs thought they were doing the right thing. They couldn't understand where we were coming from, and I know I certainly couldn't see where they were coming from. In the end we both thought we were honoring God with our actions. We'll probably never know this side of heaven who was right—maybe them, maybe us, or maybe both.

Without years of growth and self-reflection, I never could have written that last paragraph. I certainly couldn't have done it during that cover controversy with *Payable on Death*. That one pissed me off more than any of the others because to me it was personal. If you remember, my mom was all about butterflies. They were sewn onto her clothes, embedded into her jewelry, hanging from our walls. One picture that was especially dear to her was an art nouveau drawing that appeared on the February 2, 1922, edition of *Life* magazine. Called "The Flapper," it depicted a dancer who had transformed into a butterfly and had the magazine's name, *Life*, in bold letters at the top. The word fit perfectly, because for my family butterflies symbolized life, and this beautiful work of art depicted the joy of being alive. When my mom died, I took that picture, and now it's hanging in my own home.

After our boy-band-looking cover for *Satellite*, we wanted to go back to being creative and artsy. We gave that butterfly picture to Daniel Martin Diaz, a great artist known for his Catholic symbolism and ethnic feel. What he came back with was breathtaking. Once you lay your eyes on this angelic butterfly-woman, it's difficult to pull them away.

"Wait! She's half-naked! We can't have that in our Christian bookstore where little Timmy and Johnny might see it. They might be tempted to lust!" Yeah, dude, but you can't see anything. "A pubic bone! I can see her pubic bone!" It's one miniscule line in an entire piece of art! If that album cover is the gateway picture that will lead your sons down the rabbit hole to debauchery, then you need to reevaluate your parenting.

The controversy raged. But we were done with giving in to the complaining, as was the label. There was no way in hell that we were going to alter the cover in any way this time. As a result, 85 percent of Christian bookstores refused to carry the album.

Whatever.

Maybe it was because we were so over the cover crap that we later missed the blunder with *Testify*. The title of the album spreads across the entire top half of the cover. The font has a bit of a Latin/gothic feel, and the middle letter is enlarged to twice the size of those on either side. Unfortunately, that middle letter was a "T." Here we were, determined to let folks know that we are a rock band who happens to be Christian rather than a Christian band who happens to rock, and we put out an album with a cross as the centerpiece of its cover. It was the most blatantly Christian cover of any of our albums. By the time we noticed, it was too late.

At least the Christian bookstores didn't complain about that one. Apparently, for little Timmy and Johnny, crosses are safer than pubic bones any day of the week.

THE VIDEO FOR "WILL YOU" hit number one on *TRL*'s Top Ten and stayed on the list for a while. It seemed that *Payable on Death* was on the same trajectory as *Satellite*. When it finally came time for that incredible video for "Change the World" to drop, we waited. And we waited. There was nothing. It was then that we were clued in to the apocalypse that was taking place at Atlantic and within the rest of the record industry.

We had built personal relationships with our team at Atlantic. Half of them had stayed at my Noni's house after 9/11 because they couldn't get flights back to New York. We were like family. But now we came to find out that most of our team was gone. Those that were left were shell-shocked. Walking zombies. They were just waiting to be fired.

When we finally found our "Change the World" video, it was still sitting on the desk of one of the P.O.D. team at Atlantic. She hadn't submitted it to MTV. She hadn't sent it anywhere. In fact, none of the rest of our songs even got submitted to radio anywhere. We were one of the biggest artists the previous year at Atlantic, and they didn't work our record at all.

So, we did what we always do. We hit the road. If they weren't going to get our record out, we would. We did a huge summer tour with Linkin Park, Hoobastank, and Story of the Year. Everywhere we went, the arenas sold out. Later we played a bunch of shows with Staind. We toured and toured and forced people to take notice of our new album. *Payable on Death* went gold in the States and probably sold over a million worldwide. But it wasn't near the success that we thought we were going to have. We had done all we knew how to do. But behind the scenes, the labels were crumbling, and the music industry was transforming.

QUITE HONESTLY, I believe that the bigwigs at Atlantic were smugly looking at the sales of *Payable on Death* and thinking, *Yeah, that's that Christian band. We already got way more than we expected from them, but we always knew there's no way they'd sustain.* They never believed in us, because the bias against anything even remotely Christian is so strong. Like I said before, Christian music is automatically B-listed. Sadly, that's not just in label boardrooms; that's throughout the world.

Undoubtedly, there is a lot of cheesy crap put out from the Christian industry. We've already talked about that. So much in Christian music is overly dramatic and excessive. It's like there's a contest to see who can say the name "Jesus" the most in their songs. When I step back from my church self and try to hear the music from an average person's ear, I can see why they run away from it. It's all "blood of the lamb" and "living sacrifice" and other bizarre-sounding phrases. Without carrying your pocket glossary of Christian phrases, it just sounds weird and cultish.

But the bias goes beyond quality. It's the inherent message that drives people away. Admittedly, I am slipping into a spiritual argument here, but music promoting goodness and sacrifice and hope goes completely against the world's system. Slipping the name "Jesus" just once into your lyrics will have people reaching for the skip button. It is an anti-religious, anti-Christian prejudice that most people don't even know they have. Even though P.O.D. wasn't a Christian rock band, we were guilty by association. So, why should the execs at Atlantic feel compelled to push our music? They already got the better end of the deal when it came to my band. Sure, they were contractually committed to drop another million-and-a-half into producing our next record. But once that baby was born, there was no one left at the label who had the desire or responsibility to feed it and help it grow.

Once again, we knew that we were on our own. This band was going to be what we made it. After doing some promotion with Jason in Europe and headlining Edgefest in New Zealand, we ended up on that cool run with Staind that I mentioned. That's where we met the Flyleaf camp, who were opening up the show. They came up to us and said, "Dude, we're Christians. We love you guys!" We ended up spending that whole tour getting to know them, letting them know all the cool stuff to expect, warning them about the jaded side of things and all the pitfalls they would likely face. It was funny, when we first met them they were super Christianese—"Hallelujah, brother" and that kind of thing. Usually, that's a huge red flag to me. But I could see that these were just green kids who had grown up in the church. There was nothing disingenuous about them. Besides, these kids could play!

So, I did what I could to wean them into the rock and roll life. When we'd go and have card night with Taproot and Staind, I'd make sure they were invited. Not only did I want Flyleaf to get a feel for these other bands, but I wanted the other bands to see that Flyleaf wasn't some weird, afraid-of-their-own-shadows group of kids. I loved that band, and Lacey Sturm is still like a little sister to me.

Going back to what I was just saying about the bias, one thing I wanted to make sure Flyleaf understood was that they needed to be ten times better than any other band. You absolutely must build the credibility. That way, people can talk all the trash they want about our Jesus, but when we go up there and murder the stage, they can't say nothing. That was our great equalizer.

There are plenty of Christian bands that suck and everyone in the room knows that they suck. But because you're a Christian, you're obligated to say, "Well, bless their hearts. They're doing it for the Lord. Now, let me go buy one of their overpriced CDs in the foyer." But the realists and the non-Christians, they're like, "What? These guys blew!"

It all comes down to the music. The music is undeniable. You kill the stage and there's no room for "Oh, they suck because they're Christians." If anything, with P.O.D., we flipped it. "Dude, did you see those guys? They killed it. And did you know they're Christians?" They have to acknowledge the music.

It's like driving past Luis's Mechanic Shop, and down on the corner of his sign he has a little Christian fish symbol. I see that and think, "You know, Luis, I really don't care if you're a Christian or not. I want you to fix my car so that it doesn't stall on the freeway when I'm with my kids." But people use the fish to say, "Oh, trust me. I'm one of you. Give me your business." That doesn't work for me. I'm like, "Dude, let me see your track record. If you're not proven, I'm not going to put the life of my kids into your sketchy hands. I'll trust the BBB before I trust your little fish."

We played to prove that fish or no fish, we were worth listening to. The best compliment that I could get was "Dude, P.O.D. effing rocks!" Or, even, "Dude, I hate God, but I love P.O.D." That's awesome, because if you keep listening, I believe sooner or later, you'll be loving God.

But no matter how hard we played and how good the music was, we could never prove ourselves to the Atlantic execs. We would always be B-listers to them. So, even though they were about to throw a million-and-a-half dollars at us to produce *Testify*, there was no one left at the label who gave a damn enough to promote the music.

11

SEPARATE WAYS

Our time with Atlantic Records was rapidly coming to a close. We just didn't know it yet. Sure, we were skeptical of the label. But maybe it really was just a glitch in the system. The record industry had taken a massive nose-dive, but it had to level out sometime. Still, our distrust of Atlantic went beyond general industry problems. We suspected that they were done with us. If that were true, then we were fully prepared to be done with them. But that was a decision for another time. We had a record to make.

A change of pace was needed, so we rented a couple houses in Palm Springs. Truby and his family took one house. Traa, Wuv, and I took the other. It seems every house in Palm Springs has some sort of rock and roll history to it. Ours had a true vibe. It was owned by John Phillips of the Mamas and the Papas, and it was wild picturing him and his wife, Michelle, lounging around the pool creating music with Denny Doherty and Mama Cass.

Travis Wyrick flew in to work with us in the early stages. Travis is a genuine guy and a dear friend. We cleared the living room of all the furniture, set up our equipment, and just started jamming and writing. It was a good feel, and the songs poured out. Everything we did was captured by Travis, and we ended up using a bunch of his stuff in the final album.

The whole time we were in Palm Springs, we were living it up. We had this huge house. The homies were coming up from Southtown and hanging. There were three casinos around just begging to take our money. I know for Truby, it was a whole different experience with his wife there. But she was what he needed to keep him on the straight. Living the crazy rock and roll life was leading him down some paths where he knew he shouldn't be. Having family near helped keep him sane.

Finally, all the tunes were written and recorded. The plan was to send them to the label, then hook up with our producer, who would flesh out the music. The dude we wanted to work with was Greg Fidelman. He had done a lot of engineer work with bands like Red Hot Chili Peppers, System of a Down, and Slipknot, and now he was getting more into producing. We met up in Sausalito, just across the Golden Gate Bridge from San Francisco, at a studio called The Plant.

Dude, we were stoked to be going to this studio. The Plant's brand had been around since the late sixties, and it seemed that every group and artist you can think of had recorded at their New York, LA, or Sausalito studios. The alumni of the northern California studio where we were headed included Stevie Wonder, Prince, Metallica, John Fogerty, Carlos Santana, and the list goes on.

We walked into The Plant with these high hopes. But it turned out to be a huge mess. First of all, the studio was grungy. Old, run-down, a little mangy, it was obvious that it was on its last legs. In fact, the only record I could find that came out of the Sausalito studio after we were there was The Fray's self-titled album in 2009. So, we were definitely at the tail end of the Bay Area Plant's history.

But it was more than just the studio. Even though Fidelman was a good guy, we just weren't connecting. We were trying to keep the vibe going from Palm Springs—in the studio all day and having our fun at night. But it just wasn't working, and we didn't know why.

We took a break from the record, hoping that a quick breather could get the vibe going. Our focus switched to recording "Payback," the main track for the movie *XXX: State of the Union*. Fidelman did a great job on that song. But once we got back to work on *Testify*, we recognized pretty quickly that it wasn't going to work.

And it wasn't just us. Rubeli wasn't feeling it either. And when we sent the tracks to the label, they made it clear that they also weren't feeling it. It was just some intangible gap between good and great that neither Fidelman nor we could seem to leap.

It was time to shift to Plan B. We still had the recordings that Travis had done. What we didn't have was more budget. John Rubeli stepped in and convinced the label to drop us some more money. Then, Atlantic went a step further.

They gave us money for a new producer. And not just *a* producer. They gave us enough money for *the* producer.

Producer extraordinaire—Mr. Glen Ballard!

If you know even a little about the recording industry, then it is likely that the heavens opened up and a choir of heavenly angels began singing at the mention of Glen Ballard's name. He's worked with everyone. Michael Jackson, Van Halen, the Goo Goo Dolls. Hell, he flat out created Alanis Morissette. Dude's house is filled with Grammys, most of which are just stuffed on a shelf collecting dust. And I know they're there firsthand because his house is where we went to record. Or, at least, it was a studio in a house that he called Aerowave.

You might think that with a history and reputation like Glen's, he would come with an ego. But he was the nicest, most down-to-earth guy. He welcomed us into his home and into his daily routine. We would get there in the morning and record all day with him. Then, at night we'd have dinner. And with Glen, dinner was always an event.

When the time came to eat, we'd walk out of the studio and into the kitchen, where our candlelit dinner was set. We'd gather around the table with him and his other guests, which would often include his assistant, anyone there from his team, and any other random folks whom he'd either invited or who just decided to stop by. The delectable cuisine was always prepared by a chef friend or delivered from one of the finest local restaurants.

Every night, the meal would last two to two-and-a-half hours. In our glasses would be this expensive Napa Valley wine called Chateau Montelena, while he contented himself with his big, old water glass. Then after our amazing dinner, it was time to jam. Glen's an unbelievable pianist. Jason wasn't with us at that time since we were mostly doing ambient stuff, so we had brought in a gifted guitar player named Joel Shearer. Every night, with everyone feeling a little mellow after dinner and the Napa wine, Traa, Wuv, Joel, and Glen would start jamming, going late into the evening. I'd just sit there with my glass and soak in the front row view of this incredible work of living musical art. It was also during those times that it became obvious that Glen's big, old water glass at dinner was filled with vodka, so that by the time dinner and work were over, he was ready to jam and have some fun. Our time at Aerowave was quite possibly the best experience I ever had recording.

"ROOTS IN STEREO" was our lead song on *Testify*, and it's still one of my favorite songs to play. We knew about this Jewish guy out of Brooklyn who was doing reggae music, and we dug his vibe. He had a long beard and was decked out in his full-on Orthodox gear. Most definitely unique. We needed this kid. He didn't have any studio records out at the time, just a live album. But we knew he was signed to a label. I put Rubeli on the case, and he tracked down a number for Matisyahu.

He was in Israel when I called him. I told him, "Dude, we've got this track, and we need you on it." He was all in. We set everything up for him when he came to Aerowave. Made sure there were kosher meals for him and places available when it was time for him to cut out and do his prayers.

When you listen to "Roots in Stereo," you'll hear that I had him do all the fills, but I also gave him the bridge. He wrote it right there on the spot, and when he laid it down, it was flawless. Such a cool moment!

There were certainly differences in our understanding of who God is, but we were both making our music for a higher purpose. In the band, we laughed thinking about how this would blow the minds of some of the ultra-uptight branch of the church folk. We got enough flak from them for being Christians and playing what they considered to be Rastafarian religion music. Now we'd taken it up a notch. We added a Hasidic Jew, and together we were all doing the demon reggae.

Matis killed "Roots," but it was a rock song. We wanted to let him go full reggae. That's how "Strength of My Life" was born. He took Psalm 27 and rearranged a few words, and we freestyled the whole song. Later on, I went back in and tuned up my part. But it was essentially just us jamming with our voices the way Glen and the band were jamming with their instruments.

We loved the way that "Roots" turned out so much that we wanted it to be our first single and video. Matis was going to join us, and everything was set up for it to be shot among the Hasidic community on his home turf of Brooklyn. But then we heard that someone on his label didn't like someone on our label, and they refused to let Matis participate in the video. These are the stupid games that record companies play. I told him, "Dude, they're playing a game with you. They need you right now. If you let them control you at the beginning, they'll always control you."

A couple weeks later, Rubeli called us and said that Matis was officially out. I don't blame the guy. He was nervous. You don't know what you don't know. I wish, though, that he would have stuck to his guns. By him pulling out, that meant that "Roots" was off the table as a single.

INTO THE PLACE OF "ROOTS" stepped "Goodbye for Now." This was a ballad that we never expected to highlight. It was a good record song, but it didn't really have our typical drive. But that's the song the label chose.

While touching up "Goodbye for Now" with Glen, we all agreed something was missing. We could hear it; Glen could hear it. We needed one more element to get it to the single level. We suggested to Glen that maybe a female voice in the chorus would do the trick. Often, recording is like cooking. If your meal needs a little more spice, you use what you have in the kitchen.

Our brother Sick Jack from Psycho Realm had been hanging out a lot with us at Aerowave. He was from LA and would just kick it with us because, like us, he liked the classy studio treatment provided by Mr. Ballard. Hell, we were all just guys from the hood, and here's this dude feeding us and putting expensive wine out on the table. Who wouldn't want to post up?

Since the homie Jack was always with us, you know we had to have him bless a track. Along with Jack, we asked our Samoan "uncles," the legendary Boo-Yaa T.R.I.B.E., to get down as well. They came over for the studio experience, we broke bread, and "On the Grind" was born. Rest in Peace Uso, Ganxsta Ridd.

For "Goodbye for Now," Glen happened to have the perfect voice hanging around. He told us about a new protégé he was working with. He'd bring her over, and if we liked her, we liked her. If not, no big deal. We're like, "Dude, cool with us. I mean, you're Glen Ballard, right?"

So, he invited her over. She walked in and we saw this cute girl, about twenty years old. Definite punk vibe, very tomboy. Glen said, "Let me introduce you to Katy Perry." We all hit it off. Sweet girl. She had heard of us and was anxious to show us the Jesus tattoo on her wrist that she had gotten a couple years before.

Katy began hanging around the dinners for our "family time," which is exactly what it felt like. Her voice, particularly at the end of the song, added an amazing dimension to "Goodbye for Now." When it came time to shoot the video, she joined us. The video became our fourth to hit *TRL*'s number one spot. Later, when we were invited onto *The Tonight Show with Jay Leno*, she was onstage with us, as was Glen. People who were watching were probably wondering who the cute girl with the pipes and the old dude on the keyboards were. Little did they know, one was a legend and the other would soon become one.

Katy did a Mountain Dew show with us and a few others. But when her song "I Kissed a Girl" came out, she had plenty enough of her own career to keep her busy. As soon as I heard that song, I knew she was going to blow up. It was a perfectly planned controversy and planted her squarely in the spotlight. At some point, she and Glen had a falling-out. But she had already connected with óur old Atlantic publicist, the late Angelica Cob-Baehler. Angelica was brilliant at what she did, and she took Katy to the moon.

OUR SECOND SINGLE from *Testify* was "Lights Out." It was the hard guitar, heavy bass, rap metal blast that all the Warriors expected from P.O.D. We turned to Estavan Oriol for the video. Estavan was an LA-based street photographer who had started branching into videos, putting out works for Limp Bizkit, Cypress Hill, and some others. We were connected through so many people on the West Coast that we were bound to collab together at some point. We brought him to New York, and he took us outside and did the shoot in Times Square.

Right at the beginning of the video, we come rolling up in this sweet black convertible Pontiac Solstice. That was us totally going Hollywood! We had started a relationship with the head marketing guy from Pontiac, Dino Bernacchi, and that was flat-out product placement. That's right, dude, we took Pontiac's money to the bank. With the Atlantic shaft, we grabbed cash wherever we could get it. And if you think that is selling out to the man, then you know absolutely nothing about the business of rock and roll.

But Pontiac was cool with us. We ended up playing the Pontiac Garage New Year's Eve in Times Square for a couple years in a row. First year was with Truby. The second was with Marcos. The best thing to come out of that deal was a friendship with Dino that still lasts to this day.

We were still doing the formula with *Testify*, the same routine that got us to the top. But we weren't feeling the love at all anymore from Atlantic. We wanted family. They were just business. And the way they were handling that business sucked. John Rubeli was doing all he could to keep together what little relationship was left with the label, but it was a hopeless task. The love was gone, our family was dead; it was time for a divorce.

Atlantic still owed us a million-and-a-half-dollar budget to record the next album. That was our money to do with what we pleased. We could have spent twenty bucks slapping out some songs and pocketed the rest, but that's not how we rolled. However, we also knew that we didn't want to put our hearts and souls into another record and have them do jack with it again. So, we made a deal. You guys keep the money, but you let us out of our contract.

They agreed.

But with a caveat. They wanted a greatest hits record. We're like, "Greatest hits? We've only had two really successful records in the years we've been with you, then you bozos let the next two dangle in the wind. Besides that, we haven't been around long enough to be doing a greatest hits album already. Who do you think we are? The Eagles? The Doobie Brothers?" But they just wanted to try to make that extra buck off us before they happily sent us on our way.

Whatever. If that's the price for us to be done with you guys, then go for it. Atlantic wanted to add two new songs, so they could promo it with a single. I really dug the first one, called "Here We Go." We did it with Glen Ballard, and it has a good vibe to it. But the label didn't hear it as a single.

For the second song, we went full circle and ended up back with Travis Wyrick, the dude with whom we started the whole *Testify* process. He had a house studio set up in Knoxville, Tennessee, so we flew back there and recorded two songs. One of the songs was called "Murder One." It was a killer song. Hardcore metal rap. And the lyrics? They were fire. Even now when I listen to it, I get pumped up. We loved it. Label said, "Too rappy. The market is over the whole rap/rock thing." We're like, "The hell it is! You guys ever hear of Linkin Park? They're top of the charts and are more rap/rock than us." The song never even made it on the disc or any disc. If you haven't heard "Murder One," check it out on YouTube.

WE ENDED UP USING "Going in Blind" for the single. We had laid down the track for the song when we were in Knoxville that first time but weren't able to finish it. Traa, Wuv, and I went back for a quick weekend with Travis to clean things up and knock out the vocals. When we got there, I was a little stressed because I still didn't have a feel for all the lyrics.

Travis invited over some neighbors of his one night. Before they got there, he told us their story. A couple weeks earlier, they had gone out, leaving their kid at their house with the grandma who was living with them. While they were gone, someone broke in and ended up murdering the grandmother and their child. We were floored.

They arrived, and, dude, there are just no words. You can't give someone who's gone through that the standard,

"Oh, bless your heart. But don't worry, God's in control. He's got a plan." So, we just loved on them, prayed with them, said what little we could come up with. They seemed to appreciate it, but it was obvious that they were still in shock. When they left, we sat there. We were all daddies. We started talking about how anyone could find the strength to go on.

I know there are some people who can just roll through tragedies. You know, it's like a guy who gives the eulogy at his son's funeral. "People need to hear the gospel, and if they're ever going to really listen to me, this is the time." Man, if that's you, more power to you. You're a superhero, dude.

I know that I'm not strong enough. I pray that God doesn't believe in me enough to test me like that. I'm telling you right now, Lord, that if you do, I'm going to fail. So, please don't bother trying. Imagine being Job from the Bible. God said to the devil, "Take all he has and test him within an inch of his life. Dude will stand for Me." So, the devil does it, and Job stands strong. It would totally suck to have God believe in you that much.

When you listen to the song "Going in Blind" or watch the video, you'll get a feel for the pain of that couple. You'll understand that idea of knowing that God is there and that He loves you. But life is lived in a fog of war. Most of the time, we don't know what the hell is going on. So, all we can do is trust that even though we can't see what's happening, God can. And when we follow Him, we know that He loves us enough to walk with us through the nightmares that sometimes become reality in this screwed-up world.

OUR TIME WITH ATLANTIC had come to an end. But that wasn't our only separation. The rock star life hadn't been easy for Jason. I'm not going to get into the details of his struggles. Those are for his book. I can't imagine trying to navigate the deep waters he was thrown into the moment he signed the papers to become part of P.O.D. He probably handled it as well as anybody could, meaning he found his way back out still married and without some sort of life-destroying addiction.

When the time came to start working on a new album, Jason called me up. "Bro, I know we're supposed to do another record," he said to me. "But I don't think I can do it. I mean, I could selfishly be there for recording it. But then it's got to be toured, and I'm not doing that again."

I've got so much respect for him making that decision. He could have kept the not touring a secret, banked the money for recording the record, then dropped the bomb on us when it was time to go on the road. Or, he could have gone back out on tour, saying, "Screw my marriage. Screw my family. Screw my Christianity. I'm a rock star." Instead, he knew what was most important, and he stepped out with integrity.

When Truby told me he was out, I was like, "I totally get it, bro." Last thing I was going to do was try to keep the dude from doing what he felt God was telling him to do. Reality was, though, that him leaving meant P.O.D. was once again without a guitar player.

Wasn't it a convenient little coincidence that I had just recently received a call from a certain former member of the band who was interested in getting together with the guys and talking?

12

CIRCUIT OVERLOAD

Have you ever had one of those moments of peace when everything seemed right in the world? Nothing to stress about. Nothing dragging you down. The future looks hopeful, but you're feeling so good in the now that you're in no rush to get there. It's like life has given you a pool, a floating lounger, an icy drink with a tiny umbrella, and all afternoon to rest. The night the band imploded, it felt like God was whispering in my ear, "Here you go, Sonny. Now you can finally relax."

But the problem with moments of peace is that they are just that—moments. Before you know it, life cannonballs your vibe and you find yourself with your drink spilled and your lounger overturned, and you're treading water in the deep end of the pool.

IT WAS HALLOWEEN NIGHT. I was up in my bathroom getting ready to take my kids trick-or-treating. My phone rang, and I answered it.

"Hey man," I heard.

I almost dropped the phone. It was Marcos. I hadn't talked to him in forever. The grapevine had kept me up with his life—his comings and goings, his ups and downs with his band, his divorce from his wife. I felt for him in those times when I knew he was struggling. Still, I never picked up the phone to call him. I don't know, man. I just couldn't bring myself to do it, and I didn't figure he'd want to hear from me anyway.

Now here he was. I managed to get out, "What's up, dude? How's it going?"

"Not much happening, man, I just miss my friends."

Humble. Laid back. I've got to give it to Marcos, he was the bigger man. He made the connection. We spent a little time catching up, only briefly talking about the band and the breakup. One event he did bring up was the murder of Dimebag Darrell of Pantera from a couple years earlier. Dimebag was the guitarist for the band Pantera and a sweetheart of a guy. After Pantera broke up, he and his brother, Vinnie Paul, formed a new band called Damageplan. One night when they were performing, a crazy Pantera fan, upset at the band's breakup, jumped onstage and started firing. Four were killed, including Dimebag. Marcos said that when he heard about that, it messed him up for a while. "You guys are my brothers," he said. "If that kind of thing ever happened . . ."

WUV, TRAA, AND I, along with Tim Cook, met up with Marcos for lunch. Man, it was sweet. Nothing stressful. It was all just easy as we caught up with each other. We didn't tell him about Truby being gone, and he never brought up wanting to get back into the band.

As we were wrapping up, Marcos gave each of us a book on U2—kind of like their story. It was perfect. U2 was like *the* band for us. We had so much respect for them. They were somehow able to separate their Christianity from their music, but in a good way. They were positive in what they played, just like we tried to be. But they had somehow achieved that singular place of being an incredible rock group made up mostly of Christians, who played Christianish songs, and they did it without being tagged as being a Christian band. In other words, what we strove to be, they nailed.

For some reason that battle between the Christian and secular was always tough for us. When I look back now, I wonder how much of the responsibility for that struggle fell on me. As the frontman, I felt responsible for keeping us on mission. I don't think staying on track was ever as strong a conviction for the rest of the guys. That's not a knock on them. They were living their lives and their convictions. But I remember those moments of clarity when I would realize that we weren't always on the same page. It would really upset me. But that's because I was only looking through my own eyes.

Like with Marcos, I wasn't taking into account his own history growing up in an ultrareligious family. He wanted to play guitar and listen to Megadeth and Metallica. His mom would be like, "No, hijo, check out this album from

Petra instead." For him, it was like, "Yeah, they're cool, but they aren't me."

His story is the same as millions of kids who heard from their parents and their churches, "You've got to burn all your music! This is evil!" I even got some of it. I remember when Wuv and I got a whupping for listening to "Stairway to Heaven." It makes sense why so many people get turned off to that judgmental side of Christianity. My goal was to let those who had been burned by church and religion know that there is another bunch of us Christians who don't care what you look like or what you listen to. We love you and we know a God who very much loves you too.

Ultimately, we all wanted to inspire people. That was our common theme. We just had diverse definitions of what that meant. If we had realized that truth twenty years ago, P.O.D.'s history probably would have looked a lot different.

IT WAS A GREAT AFTERNOON for the five of us, and we left it with, "Let's do this again." We had already set up our practice studio at the old Tribal Streetwear warehouse, and we had signed with our new label, INO, which was a sublabel of Columbia. But we didn't tell Marcos right off about Truby. We didn't know what we wanted when it came to him and the band, and we didn't want him to feel any pressure. So, we just played it slow. At some point after meeting up again, we said to Marcos, "Hey, we've got all our stuff set up. If you ever feel like stopping by and jamming for old times' sake . . ." He was like, "Really? Yeah, all right." It was all very cool, very natural.

So we jammed together, and it was a beautiful thing. We could totally feel that Marcos energy, that Marcos vibe. It had been great with Truby. Two different players, both brilliant in their own right. But when we started playing our old stuff with Marcos, it was like riding a bike or putting on an old shoe. It all fit just right. We goofed for hours and left it saying, "Dude, anytime you want to come by and jam."

It didn't take long before we had the conversation with Marcos. "Just so you know, Truby isn't coming back by his own choice. Think about it." We had to write and record soon, so thankfully he didn't think long. The band was back together.

I don't know that there was ever a time when I thought Marcos would never come back. But a lot had to happen. There was a lot of anger and sadness that had to be processed. Because we didn't rush it and waited on God's timing, when it did happen, it was natural and easy. When I look back now, it's hard not to see God's hand in it. He put it in Truby's heart to step out of P.O.D., while at the same time moving Marcos to reconnect. Those were two major moves that had to happen at precisely the right time and in the right way.

Some people would just say, "Coincidence." But coincidences are for those who lack the imagination to see the bigger picture.

WHEN WE WERE PLAYING, it was back to how it used to be. It was those relationship moments in between the music that, of necessity, took on a new feel. I realized that I had to be careful not to fall back into that big brother mentality. I needed to let Marcos be who he was. And when I saw him doing stuff that in the past I would have called him out on, I had to learn to shut up and let him be himself. This was for his sake and for mine. If I went back to questioning why he was doing some of the things he was doing, it would have left him pissed off and me bitter and angry. I had my mission, and he had his mission. The two intersected at a lot of points. But where they didn't, we both had to back off and just let it be.

We were looking for a producer for our next record. Marcos had a good relationship with a guy named Jay Baumgardner, and he threw his name out. Jay had a long résumé working with bands like Evanescence, Helmet, and Alien Ant Farm. I had worked with him once on a hurricane relief project and agreed that he'd do great.

Rather than posting up in the Oakwoods for our time recording, we stayed on Sunset Boulevard in Pauly Shore's house. Yeah, that Pauly Shore. His mom, Mitzi, owned and ran the famous Comedy Store with a few other people, including Pauly. If you go right behind the Comedy Store, there's a gate. Through that gate is Pauly's house. During the day, we'd go record in North Hollywood at Jay's NRG Studios. Then at night we'd go watch all these new comics. It was great, just like old times. Living back in the luxuries.

ONCE WE WERE PRETTY MUCH FINISHED with the tracks, Traa and Marcos headed home. I needed to wrap up the lyrics and the vocals, so there was a lot of time I was there by myself. Wuv stuck around too, but he was out doing his thing most of the time, so I didn't see him much. I guess he figured he had already done his part. Now it was time for fun. After all, we were in Hollywood.

It's not my place nor my intention to expose anyone's struggles or faults. We all have them. In the Bible, the apostle Paul wrote, "Christ Jesus came into the world to save sinners—and I am the worst of them all" (1 Tim. 1:15). Dude, that is so right on, and that's how I feel. Anytime I'm talking about anyone else's struggles, I'm doing it as someone who understands my own place as "the worst of them all."

I knew my cousin had been going through some tough times in his life and that it was becoming obvious to more than just me. Out of love and concern for him, I felt I needed to confront him. His bedroom was in a whole different part of Pauly's house, so late one night I walked over there to talk. I'll give it to him; he came clean on everything. I reminded him what was at stake for him, for his family, for his spiritual life if he kept on the same path. It was a good talk, and I felt like he was really listening to me. Sadly, I was wrong.

Watching him crash put me in a dark place. We had always been navigating this rock star life together, trying to figure it out as we sometimes teetered on that line of what's too far, what's too much. But we always had this mentality of "Dude, none of us will ever cross that line because we love God. We have conviction." But what was happening with Wuv at that time was bound for a crash and burn.

When you listen to *Angels & Serpents Dance*, musically it's not the darkest or heaviest album. But when you really take in the lyrics, there are a lot of dark and heavy moments. You can hear the burden that I was carrying. It wasn't intentional, like I'm venting my frustration through the music. It was all subconscious, spurring from simply being in the moment.

Typically, during the tough times of recording, I knew that I at least had the weekends to come home and decompress. But during this time, I didn't even have that. Shannon was awesome as always, but she was also eight months pregnant with my son. Then, just to add another punch to the gut, her dad was diagnosed with cancer. I can remember him coming to me to let me know, then telling me not to say anything to Shannon. He didn't want her carrying that worry into her final months of pregnancy. So, that was one more pain that I had to stuff down inside. *Keep a smile on your face, Sonny. Keep pushing forward, Sonny. Remember, everyone is counting on you—your wife, your family, the band.*

The weight was getting unbearable.

I HAD FINISHED UP RECORDING one Friday. After hanging around the studio until eight or nine o'clock to let the LA traffic calm, I took off by myself for the drive home. All the crap of the band and life were swirling around in my brain and weighing on my heart. By the time I hit the halfway point, I started feeling weird—foggy. It was like I was high, but not a good-feeling high.

I pulled into a gas station to get some water. Inside, I found myself cruising the aisles, aimlessly looking at stuff, trying to figure out this funky head change I was experiencing. Home was only about an hour and a half away, so I called Shannon, told her I wasn't feeling right, and let her know my ETA. The rest of the trip I kept my truck in the slow lane with the windows down. When I finally made it home, Shannon was waiting. I crashed for the night.

The next day, I still felt sick and a little weird. Even on Sunday at church, as I was watching the pastor, I was feeling claustrophobic in the big auditorium. That afternoon, we went to the movies, and I felt like I was trapped in a box. It wasn't until later that I figured out that I must have been having a panic attack. I'd never experienced that before, and I haven't since. I knew that something had to change.

A few weekends later, my family and I were sitting outside, playing in the pool. Shannon was due any day. I was watching them while my mind raced. Then a thought hit me, and I knew what I needed to do. I went and got our camera. When I came back, I asked Shannon to take some pictures of me and the girls by the pool. They were still little—Nevaeh had just turned seven and Marley was about to be three. It was a beautiful, sunny summer SoCal day, and we were laughing and playing. I was throwing my dreads on them, and they were pretending it was their hair. Shannon, though, was getting suspicious as she was snapping pictures. She knew something was up.

Then I asked my oldest, "Hey, Nevaeh, take a picture of me with Mommy." I leaned into Shannon, and my daughter snapped a picture. I ducked down and threw my dreads over her belly. The girls laughed, but my wife was giving me a look. I told them, "Hang on." I went inside the house and came back out with a pair of scissors. "Shannon, I want you to cut the first dread," I said to my wife. Then turning to my daughters, I said, "Nevaeh, you cut the second, and, Marley, you cut the third."

They started tripping. "Daddy, we love your dreads! Don't do it!"

Them crying didn't help me at all because I was already on the verge of bawling. It had been twelve years since I had cut my hair. The dreads were down past my butt. And it wasn't just losing the hair. The dreads were who I was. It's how people recognized me. It's my roots. I'm a dread! But I knew it had to be done.

"It's okay," I said to my girls. "Daddy just needs to do this."

Shannon looked at me. She knew. This wasn't just some spur-of-the-moment whim. This was a necessary step in my life. Taking the scissors from my hand, she cut the first dread off. She passed the scissors to Nevaeh, who cut the second. Marley followed up with the third.

Dude.

I was so sure I was going to die with my dreads. It was a spiritual thing for me. In the Old Testament, people who wanted to commit fully to God would take what was called a Nazirite vow. Part of that commitment was not cutting your hair. Do you remember the story of Samson and Delilah? She tricked him into telling her that his strength was in his dreads. But it wasn't really in his hair. It was in the commitment he had made to God that was symbolized by his hair. When Delilah cut his dreads, it was a demonstration of his unfaithfulness.

But for me, cutting my dreads was the opposite. I had lost myself in the band. My faith was lukewarm, and I was in danger of Sonny the rock star overtaking Sonny the father and the follower of God. Getting rid of my hair was like stripping myself of the world and all its pull. It was me laying myself bare before God and saying, "This is me, your kid. Take the band. Take the fame. Take the money. I want to be a husband, a father, and a follower of you—nothing more." My dreads were my offering to God to show him that I was serious.

WHEN I GOT BACK TO NORTH HOLLYWOOD, Jay and everybody tripped out. Then Marcos and Traa came in and they freaked. Everybody wanted to know why. But it was too fresh to go into detail, too personal. I just told them I needed a change. Wuv had been MIA lately, so he was the last to see. When he did finally show up, it was with a bunch of people we didn't know. I don't know, man. It was just awkward. He had the whole "Whoa, what the heck" reaction, but it was just the wrong time and the wrong place, and his head was in the wrong space.

I don't want it to come across like the whole *Angels & Serpents Dance* sessions were downers. There were some great times with the band. And we once again wanted to bring special guests onto the record. With *Testify*, we had pulled more from the hip hop pool. This album, we went back to rock and reggae legends. I had been a fan of Suicidal Tendencies since I was a teenager. We reached out to Mike Muir, even though as far as we knew he had never guest appeared on any record. But he said yes and did an amazing performance on "Kaliforn-Eye-A." What an honor.

Helmet was playing in LA while we were recording, and Marcos and I caught their show. We met and hung out with the singer, Page Hamilton, after their set. As we were talking, we toyed with the idea of him being a guest feature. Later, when we were recording vocals, we hit him up, and he agreed. It was legend.

But the experience that topped them all was when I flew down to Miami with Mark Renk, our vocal arranger, to record Cedella and Sharon Marley. I remember walking through their brother Stephen Marley's huge compound to his studio. It was like walking through little Jamaica. There were kids everywhere, and everyone was all dread-locked up. It was a crazy, beautiful vibe.

Unfortunately for me, I had cut my dreads two weeks before. I felt naked walking past everyone. Seemed like forever I grew those dreads, and the day I finally got to visit the Miami Marley compound, I looked like some crazy, baldhead heathen. God's got some hilarious timing.

Cedella was Bob and Rita's daughter, and Sharon was adopted by Bob when he and Rita got married. They and another girl named Erica Stewart were in a singing group called The Marley Girls. The sisters also made up half of The Melody Makers, along with Stephen and their other brother, Ziggy. They were so warm and friendly, and they laid down a beautiful background for the song "I'll Be Ready." Just like it had been with Mike and Page, hearing my vocals with the legendary Marley women supporting it was a dream come true.

I saw Stephen as we were walking through. He had just put out his first solo album, *Mind Control*, which was my favorite record of that year. We stopped, and I thanked him for letting us use his studio. Then I told him what I thought of his album. He was so cool, so kind. It was an amazing experience. I walked away thinking, *I was just at the freaking Marley kids' house!*

WE FINISHED THE RECORD and got ready to go back to touring. But the whole vibe with the band was different. I found myself separating from the other guys. It wasn't that I didn't like them or that I had something against them. It's just, with all the personal changes and family drama, it was hard to connect with the guys, especially my cousin. I didn't want to go on acting as if nothing had happened. I'm sure all of us could have simply swept everything under the rug, saying, "It's just rock and roll."

But no matter how much I tried, it just didn't feel the same anymore. Turning a blind eye wasn't an option this time. In the past, we'd all done what we used to label "stupid things." But those "stupid things" never hurt anybody, and life just went on. This time, though, life-altering mistakes were taking place, and I was determined not to make those same choices myself. God knows I'm no saint. My whole life, even up to that moment, I'd been facing my own demons and dealing with my own struggles.

Through all this confusion and turmoil, there was one truth that stood out crystal clear to me. I would not have survived another album cycle of touring with that "business as usual" mentality. I couldn't go on acting like nothing had happened. It felt like my world was turning upside down due to bad choices that were taking place around me. I couldn't find the strength to keep going, and I was running out of reasons why I should.

Our first time on the road after *Angels & Serpents Dance* was for a series of charity gigs with Hard Rock. Starting in Miami and ending in San Diego, we'd hit all these Hard Rock Cafes and play a set. If there were stages, we'd play the stages. If there weren't, they'd just shove all the tables to the side and we'd go punk rock style. All went fine until the final night. That's when it blew apart.

We were in San Diego, so all our loved ones and our homies showed up. We were getting ready for the show when we heard that crazy drama was taking place outside with our families. Before, we'd been able to keep family issues separate from business. But now, the drama was starting to spill into our professional lives. It was so bad that the cops were called in.

With all that going down, I remember something clicking in my mind, telling me that this would be the last show that I'd ever play with P.O.D. It was over. Everything had just hit the fan, and now it was done. Dude, let me tell you, when we played that show, I had a fire in me like I've never felt before. If this was it, I was going out in a blaze of glory. I had friends later tell me that they saw something in me they'd never seen before. One dude said, "I saw something on Sonny. I couldn't even look at his face."

I don't know what it was. Maybe it was all the sadness, gratefulness, anger, relief, all pouring out in that moment.

The drama continued after the show, but I finally got myself out of there. On the ride home, I remember thinking, *That's it. Close the chapter. I'm ready for something new, God.* We were booked to do a cross-country radio tour, driving from town to town playing our crossover song "Tell Me Why." But Tim Cook was smart, he'd figure our way out of that. It was time now for everyone to go their separate ways, work on their separate projects, work on their separate lives.

That night, I probably slept better than I ever had. I felt such incredible freedom. Yeah, we had issues in our extended family, but they weren't my problems. We'd find a way through. All the band stuff with the relationships and the mission and the temptations and the boundaries and all that never-ending crap that I had been carrying on my shoulders and that had just kept getting heavier and heavier as the years went by? Over. Done. No more. For the next two days I woke up like, "This is the best feeling in the world."

It was a moment of peace like I hadn't experienced in thirty years.

But remember, the problem with moments of peace is that they are just that—moments.

Tim Cook called. "Dude, we have this agreement for a whole radio promo run. The label really believes this is our crossover song. We said we would do it, man, we've got to follow through." Blah, blah, blah, blah, blah. And just like that, my moment was gone.

Damn.

Back on the road, hitting one radio station after another. Dude, that was one long stretch. Afterwards, we toured, but not like before. Now, we'd fly out, do a gig, then fly back home. The only video we released for the album was "Addicted." Instantly, people were asking whether it was written about anyone in particular, if maybe it had something to do with some family issues. People look to stir up crap wherever they can. Trust me, my family has felt plenty of pain from addiction. Shannon's got an addicted brother who's out on the streets somewhere. Me, I come from a family of addicts. Addiction is just one of those topics. It's reality.

We did Jay Leno and a few other things, but we all felt it crumbling within. Finally, I hit up Tim and said, "Dude, I can't anymore. I need to stop. The only way I won't quit this band right now is if I can take a break." He got a call together with Wuv, Marcos, Traa, and me and told them that we're going to take a year off. After that time, we'd meet back up and see where we were.

It was a necessary end to a very long stretch of my life. But it was exactly what I needed for God to turn the page and start a brand-new chapter.

13

WHOSOEVER WILL

Tribe.

There's something about that word that speaks to my soul. I don't know if it's my Islander roots or it's just the way my heart works. To me, tribe goes deeper than blood. It's more than family, although family can be a part. It's more than community or even friendship. Tribe says we think alike, we believe alike. We are on the same mission, moving in an identical direction. Our purposes match, our values match, our standards match. In my tribe, I can be completely real, authentic, mask off.

When P.O.D. began, Wuv, Marcos, and Traa were my tribe. We were doing life together and all moving in the same direction. But the older we got, with everything we went through—things just changed. Perspective changed. Mission changed. Purpose changed. Attitudes changed. And I'm not saying that any one perspective or mission or purpose was better than another. We all just diverged.

Although I didn't really know it at the time, one of the main reasons I needed the break from the band was that I was looking for my people. Despite all the love we had for each other in the band, I needed to find some like-minded people. What made that difficult was that I wasn't even sure where my own mind was.

When I first became a Christian, I thought that church and all the other believers in Jesus were going to be my tribe. It worked for my mom and my aunt and uncle. But it didn't take me long to realize that even if I had been interested in that mainstream brand of churchianity, a whole lot of the people sitting in their pews every Sunday weren't interested in me or folks who looked like me, talked like me, or dug the music I was into.

So, it became me and the band against the world. Me, Wuv, Traa, and Marcos lived and died for each other. We survived together. We paid all the struggling band dues with one another. But then came success, and we could finally climb up out of the foxhole. Instead of living room floors and Denny's, we had luxury hotels and gourmet cuisine. Instead of beater vans, we had buses and semis. It's the battle that unites people. Times of peace and comfort allow families to drift apart.

My tribe had drifted, which led me to the conclusion that my time with P.O.D. was likely done. I needed to know what God had for me next, but I had no clue how I was going to figure that out. I prayed, "God, show me where I can find some answers."

That's when He sent me Ryan Ries, and I said, "Really, God?"

I first met Ryan Ries through my friend Guido. It was a few years before the band hiatus, and we were hanging out one day. Guido suddenly said, "Hey, I'll take you up to C1RCA skate. I know some of the guys. They'll hook you up with some product." I was all in.

As we're going there, he's telling me that the owner was Raul Ries, Jr. I'm like, "You mean like the pastor Raul Ries? The dude who was going to kill his wife and kids but got saved?" Guido says, "Yeah, it's his son."

I remembered Raul Ries from my days growing up. My family had gotten saved in a Calvary Chapel church, so they were part of that Calvary circle. For my buddies and me, when we looked at the Calvary churches, we were thinking these dudes looked pretty white. But then we heard Raul Ries preaching with his heavy accent. Me and all my homies from my Mexican and Chicano hood were like, "Dude, check it out! They accidentally let a Mexican in through the back door!" So, Raul Ries was always cool with me, even though I had never met him.

We got to C1RCA, but Raul Jr. wasn't there. His little brother, Ryan, was. Dude, he was a mess. All skinny and sucked up, he had that look of "Yeah, this guy is living it up right now." I could tell he was in trouble. But, man, he was a sweet kid. Ryan's the kind of guy who will make you feel like you're his best friend within five minutes of meeting him.

As we talked, I was thinking, *This may be Raul Ries's son, but he's a broken man. No self-righteousness. No arrogance. Walked away from the church system, and now he's totally adrift.* Ryan was exactly the kind of guy I do well with, the kind of guy I wanted to get to know.

C1RCA got me set up with some gear, then Guido and I took off. Ryan and I didn't see each other after that for a while, but we kept in loose contact.

The band was winding up *When Angels & Serpents Dance* when we got a call to play one of Raul Ries's Somebody Loves You events. We hadn't played an evangelistic crusade event like that for a long time, and I was thinking there's no way the guys, Marcos especially, would want to do it. But Raul Ries's name had that pull for us. We figured that if it was his thing, it probably wouldn't be cheesy or kooky like a lot of crusades. So we said yes.

The date was getting nearer when I got a call from Ryan. He was like, "Hey, what's up, dude? I hear you're playing my dad's thing. Just wanted you to know that I quit C1RCA, and I've been helping my dad out." As soon as I heard his voice, I was like, "Dude's cleaned up and given his life to the Lord." He sounded so much better. But after the road he'd been on, I figured he was still broken. He had a whole lot about his life to figure out.

P.O.D. played the show, and Ryan and I caught up. He looked healthier. He'd grown his hair out a bit. It was good to see. From that time on, our phone calls became more frequent.

IT WASN'T THAT LONG AFTER when the hiatus began. Suddenly, I've got all this time on my hands with little to do other than trying to figure out my future. I'm spending my days raising my kids with Shannon, then Sundays come and I go to church. Every now and then I'd have a quick P.O.D. fly out for some commitment that had been made a while back, but other than that, there was very little band connection.

I like our pastor, but this one Sunday, man, I was in no way connecting with what he was saying. Instead, I found myself daydreaming, kind of watching him in a haze. I started focusing on the banner hanging behind him. It read "John 3:16." I think that was the first verse I ever memorized. In fact, it's still the only verse I can quote without having to give it a second thought.

> For God so loved the world, that he gave his only begotten Son, that whosoever believeth in him should not perish, but have everlasting life.

I'm there mulling over this verse when the word *whosoever* popped out at me. Whosoever believes. To me, all those whosoevers Jesus was talking about sounded like a people group. They weren't the somebodies, the Who's Who of Christianity. They weren't the ones with titles and positions and popularity. They were the nobodies and the outcasts. They were the "least of these" that Jesus talked about. This verse perfectly exposed the heart of God. "Whosoever believes" is a call to the nobodies of this world, and it's these nobodies who were my people.

In all honesty, my first thought about The Whosoevers was that it would be a really cool reggae band name. But I soon realized that it was bigger than that. What that "bigger" looked like, though, I had no clue. I certainly wasn't thinking about starting some ministry. I was so past that. To me, ministry had become a burden. Expectations were so high and so constant that it was tailor-made for burn-out. It was a ministry mindset that led me to my current floundering place with a lukewarm faith and a raging case of spiritual inadequacy. That's not where God's heart is. Jesus said that His yoke is easy and His burden is light. In other words, when you're doing what God wants you to do, it should feel smooth and natural, not forced. He wants you to love what you're doing for Him because it's so perfect for who you are.

The Whosoevers.

I knew it was something, and I had a feeling it was going to be part of my future. I just had no idea what the heck that future was going to be.

I FOUND MYSELF hanging with a youth group from this Spanish-speaking church from the neighborhood I grew up in. The youth pastors were huge P.O.D. fans, and I met them when they came up to LA for the "Goodbye for Now" video shoot. They just showed up, and we put them in. You can see them when the camera is spinning around. They're in the mix with the rest, hands up and praising the Lord. We had stayed in contact, and they invited me to the church.

It was beautiful, man. I didn't go to speak or to sing or to do anything "Sonny Sandoval." I just went to hang. At the beginning for the kids, it was like "It's Sonny from P.O.D.!" But soon they saw that I'm just another guy who was seeking the Lord like they were. "It's another Wednesday night in south San Diego, and we're here trying to love Jesus together."

Over the years, I had done a little speaking at times to different groups and churches. It wasn't long before the guys from this church were asking about putting together an event of some sort where I would share my story. I'm like, "I'm in. But let's do this thing right."

We began planning—I think we called it "Set It Off"— and I started hitting up bands I knew. When I'd tell them what was up, they were all in. I had rappers. I had a hardcore band. All were guys that I knew were Christians but out playing the secular venues and trying to make a difference. I got skaters to come in and even got Adrian Lopez to commit, because he was one of Ryan's best friends. I hit up C1RCA, Agent, Tribal Streetwear, and every other brand that sponsored P.O.D. for some giveaways and ended up with trucks full of gear to pass out.

The day came, and the church was packed. The bands were playing, and kids were everywhere skating and doing their thing. Then, at the end of the night I got up, shared my story, let them know I loved them, and asked them if there was anyone who wanted to know Jesus. I didn't know it at the time, but that event at the Southtown church was a prototype for what we'd eventually do with The Whosoevers. Don't get me wrong, people have been putting on events ever since the cavemen started banging on dinosaur skins. Ryan had been creating skate shows for years with C1RCA. All I'm saying is that this combo of music, skate, giveaway, and gospel became a hallmark for The Whosoevers in the years to come.

ONE DAY I WAS OUT TO LUNCH with my wife and kids. I got a call and stepped out to take it. Ryan was on the other end saying, "Dude, my dad and I are going to Israel. There are still spots left if you want to go." As he gave me the details, I was thinking how cool this would be. But I had to be practical. It was pricey, and at this point my family was living off my rapidly depleting savings.

I went back in and told Shannon with a laugh, "That was Ryan on the phone. He asked me if I wanted to go to Israel." Before I even finished, she said, "You've got to go." Yeah, I wasn't expecting that. I was thinking she'd be saying, "Israel? It's crazy over there right now. Besides, you're not leaving me alone again with these kids." Instead, she was like, "Sonny, you need to be there."

The timing of the trip was perfect for both Ryan and me. We were each trying to figure life out, but we were just coming at it from opposite directions. I came from outside Christianity. When I got saved, I was dragged into the whole church mindset of telling me this is what I needed to do and how I needed to act to be a good Christian. Those rules never fit me, which led me to the point I was at where I was trying to figure out how to turn my back on all those ministry-minded expectations and still be a useful follower of Jesus. Ryan, on the other hand, came from inside Christianity and at some point said, "To hell with this." He went off doing his own thing until an overdose almost killed him. Now he was trying to figure out how to fit back into the church world.

What we had in common was that both of us were trying to get back to that simple love of Jesus—what the book of Revelation called "first love." He wanted the purity of his childhood faith, and I was looking for that relationship with Jesus that I found in the hospital parking lot after my mom died. It's not that I'd turned away from my faith. But I'd experienced rock and roll to its fullest. I'd made a lot of mistakes along the way. Through it all, I never lost my convictions. I knew that the notoriety and money and luxury were all fake, and eventually it would tear me down and destroy me just like I'd seen it do to others who were close to me. When Ryan and I got on that plane, we were both in full search mode. We hoped we'd find what we were looking for on the far side of the Mediterranean.

ISRAEL WAS AMAZING. All those places I had read about in my Bible for so many years, now I was seeing them. It was like taking the black and white of all those stories and for the first time watching them in color. It was mind-blowing.

I'm a quiet guy when I'm around people I don't know. So a lot of the trip I spent sitting by myself on the bus with my headphones on soaking it all in. Ryan, though, was totally in his element. Most of the people were folks he knew from his dad's church, so he was always talking with this person and that. But when we'd get back to our room at night and debrief, it was obvious that being in this special place was working on him too. Both of us were asking the same question—Lord, what do you have for me next?

It used to be that Ryan would rather stand unarmed facing a zombie apocalypse than speak to a group of people. Dude was awesome one-on-one or just goofing off in front of a small group. But public speaking? Bring on the undead! So, I was surprised when he told me one of those late nights, "Man, even if God asked me to share my story in front of a crowd, I'd do it for Him." Then he added something like, "But I wouldn't just do it for any church or group. I've got all sorts of people wanting to hear the story of Raul Ries's prodigal son coming home. I need someone to ask me who wants to hear my story, what God's done in my life, not just in the life of Raul's druggie kid."

I totally got it. Papa Raul has a big shadow. You start out as Pastor Raul's kid, you'll always be seen as Pastor Raul's kid. It was that big shadow that made this such a huge ask. No one knew Ryan apart from his dad. To me, it sounded like he was putting up an insurmountable obstacle so that he wouldn't ever have to go through with it. If you talked to Ryan today, he'd tell you that's exactly what he was doing.

That's why it was so unbelievable when the next day he came to me and said, "Dude, I just got a call from Pastor Derek Neider in Vegas. He asked me to come speak to his church. He said he knew I have a story to tell, and he thinks people need to hear it."

Remember what I said about coincidences? Yeah, God laughs at your coincidences and says, "Just watch what I do next."

So, Ryan was kind of screwed. He gave God a big ask, and the Lord came through. Running away from something that is so clearly God doesn't tend to go well. I told him, "You never know what God's doing, man. Let's see how it goes. We'll figure it out." It wasn't long before Ryan let me know that he had it figured out. His solution was something like, "There's no way I'm doing this alone. You need to come with me."

He didn't need to convince me. I was totally down with it.

While we were still in Israel, I talked with Ryan quite a bit about The Whosoevers. He had heard about the event that I did with the Southtown church, and his mind started taking The Whosoevers that direction. I pushed back on him. "No, man, I just want a brotherhood. I'm not looking for a ministry or a bunch of events." But Ryan is an event guy. It's what he did for C1RCA. It's the way he thinks— more is better than less and bigger is better than smaller.

I think it was this "bigger is better" mindset that led him to ask me as he was preparing for his Vegas speaking debut, "Hey, you know Head, right? Think you can invite him to join us?" He had been reading Brian "Head" Welch's book and thought he might be a like-minded guy. I told him, "Yeah, I'll call him." Somehow, we also ended up getting Lacey Sturm to say she'd join us in Vegas too.

"Let's just all get together and talk about The Whosoevers." That was Ryan's reason for rounding us all up. However, I have a feeling that what came next was really his plan all along.

AFTER I LANDED IN LAS VEGAS, Ryan came driving up in a van. Inside, he already had Head and Lacey. It was beautiful, like a reunion! After we got settled into our hotel, we went to dinner at P.F. Chang's. It wasn't long before we were all feeling like we had known each other our whole lives. In a weird way, we were exactly what each other needed at the time. Head, who had left his position as guitarist for the legendary group Korn, was still working things out, trying to figure out how to be a Christian in a church culture that loved his story but would probably have been more comfortable if he had told it from behind a large pane of protective glass. Flyleaf had blown up, which meant that Lacey was dealing with a lot of the same struggles and temptations that I had dealt with, and still do.

Four followers of Jesus, at different points in their spiritual walk, living lives out of the mainstream, all trying to figure out God's plan. The world saw most of us as somebodies, but we knew better. We were just the nobodies, the confused. We wanted to be difference makers, but we didn't know how. But if there was one thing that came out of that time together in Vegas, it was that we all left committed to walking the journey together. We were The Whosoevers, and we were trusting God to bring us our tribe.

I felt so bad for Ryan when we got to the church. Dude wore a groove into the carpet with the number of times he rushed to the bathroom while he was waiting for his time to go up. But he wasn't the only one who was nervous. Somehow, he had convinced Head, Lacey, and me to share our stories too. Sneaky punk.

The time finally came, and it was Ryan raw. I had told him to be real, completely authentic, but some of the things he talked about? Dude's up there talking about being addicted to porn! There are some subjects that just aren't talked about amongst good church folk unless you're in confession mode on the final night of a men's retreat. I had no doubt that the outspoken, self-righteous, judgmental faction that you can find lurking somewhere in most churches already had their blades out and were sharpening them to a fine point.

That's the problem with so many Christians. They become jaded. It even happens to pastors. They get into the business of God and pretty soon they can't recognize a miracle even when it bites them on the ass. Ryan was a walking miracle. He was the epitome of the lost being found. But because of the way he looked or some of the things he said, people missed it. Church leaders would look down on him like, "Oh, it's just Raul's knucklehead son who got himself clean and now wants to be a pastor."

But what was beautiful were those times when he and I would speak at a church and meet the pastor. He'd be kind of stuffy and aloof, a few spiritual steps higher. Then Ryan and I would share our stories. When that pastor came back to us afterwards, he'd be completely changed. He'd have gone from being a jerk to what a pastor is supposed to be—humble and sincere. Then he'd introduce us to his son or his daughter. The kid would walk in and we'd recognize them as being the first one who stood up to give their life to Jesus after Ryan and I got done speaking. We had no idea they were the pastor's kid back in the auditorium, but we were there with our hands on their shoulders as they confessed their lives to us. God was working through us, and the pastor could finally see His hand moving when the miracle happened in his family. He'd be like, "The Whosoevers? Count me in!"

That night in Vegas was incredible. Each of us felt such freedom talking, like the Holy Spirit was giving us the words to say. We came away knowing for certain that there would be more nights to come.

BUT EVEN THOUGH we each considered ourselves to be whoso-evers, it was still just an identity rather than a formalized ministry. Ryan and I began speaking at other churches, rehabs, and youth detention centers. When we went, we did so as whosoevers but not as The Whosoevers. It was still just a brotherhood and sisterhood. That started to change a few months later at Papa Raul's next Somebody Loves You event, which took us back to Vegas. Somehow, Ryan had convinced his dad to let him take one of the two nights to put on what he called Exit. Essentially, it was going to be the same type of evangelistic event his dad was doing, but Ryan was going to update it to reach the younger unchurched.

Flyleaf was at the top of their game, and Head was making his music, so they went on the bill. I called up the Blindside guys, and they were all in. Brian Deegan and the Metal Mulisha motocross guys agreed to bring their craziness to the night. We had a couple artists who were going to be doing live paintings, then Papa Raul and I were slated to speak.

Because Somebody Loves You was such a big event, a number of the churches in Las Vegas typically banded together to help with support and promotion. The first preparation meeting that Ryan and I went to was in a ballroom at some hotel. It was packed with gray-haired church people who were so excited to have that lovely

Pastor Raul back. After the folks ate their breakfast, Raul got up and announced, "My son and Sonny Sandoval will be leading one night, and I will lead the other." Then he had us get up, and we explained what Exit was going to look like.

Let's just say that it wasn't quite what Granny Margaret and Deacon Henry had in mind. The enthusiasm and excitement that filled our description of the bands and the skaters and all the unsaved kids coming in from off the street seemed to hit an invisible seawall just before it reached the first row of round tables. But we didn't let it bother us. Whether they were in or not, Exit was going to be a night to remember.

As the events got closer, we did a follow-up breakfast. This time, though, only a handful of churches showed up. To me, this was just the same old cynical church crap I'd been dealing with for years. But it was an eye-opener for Raul and Ryan. I'll never forget during the meeting, this old lady stood up and asked, "So when these young kids give their lives to the Lord, where are they going to go?" I said to her, "Ma'am, they're going to go to your church." What a sad question that was, but I get it. She was scared. In the minds of these insulated people, they pictured a horde of drug users and heavy metallers and ungodly heathens invading their churches, loudly cussing out in the foyer, and flicking cigarette butts all over their perfectly manicured lawns.

When the time came, the Friday Exit night was packed. I think they even had to turn people away. The bands killed the stage, while Metal Mulisha was doing their thing in the parking lot. We wanted to pass out Bibles to anyone who wanted a copy. After looking at the average attendance over the past several years, they estimated that four thousand copies would be more than enough. It wasn't. When Raul asked at the end if anyone wanted to give themselves to Jesus, hands shot up, and just like that, every last Bible was gone. Dude, it was a beautiful, beautiful night.

The next day was Somebody Loves You. I don't want to knock it, because I love Papa Raul and I know that a ton of people have started a relationship with Jesus through those events. But this year, the event was nearly empty. We were shocked, but we also understood. It was designed for the same old Christian folk to have another Jesus-fest for church people. It was almost painful to watch.

When it was Raul's turn to give the message, oh man, he came with fire! He looked out at the audience, and he was pissed. Raul Ries loves the church. Ever since he got radically saved, he's been a church guy, spiritually brought up under Chuck Smith himself, the founder of Calvary Chapel. But what he saw in the churches of Vegas was a lack of urgency for those who most needed to hear that Jesus loved them. He told his listeners about the thousands who got saved the night before. "And we're just here today raising our hands in worship," he said. "The blood of the lost is on your hands."

I was on the side of the stage next to one of the other pastors at Raul's church. He had a huge smile on his face and was nudging me saying, "Now that's the Raul I know!" By the end of that weekend, Raul was fully on board with whatever God was leading The Whosoevers to become.

I WAS DETERMINED that The Whosoevers wasn't going to become just another ministry, and Ryan agreed. We both saw this as more of a movement that would shake up the world. Ryan and I spent the rest of my hiatus year speaking at different places and trying to figure out what God was doing. Raul's church, Calvary Chapel Golden Springs, was in Diamond Bar in the east Los Angeles suburbs. That's where Ryan was headquartered, and I set up shop with him there, hanging out three or four days a week. It was a long drive from my house, so a lot of nights I'd just end up crashing out on the couch in Ryan's office. Dude had a sweet couch!

It wasn't long before some folks began to joke that I was the newest staff member because I spent so much time at the church. But even though I was open to anything, I knew deep down that working there wasn't for me. I loved my time at Calvary Chapel. It was an honor to be allowed into the inner workings of the church. Still, I knew that God had put me in rock and roll and given me all those experiences and relationships for a reason. I've seen too many times when guys suddenly get this personal vision, quit their band or their acting career or whatever they were doing in the public eye, become a pastor, and fade into obscurity. And if that's truly what God calls you to, then more power to you. But I think for many it's just them running away from the temptations that come with the platform that God has given them to operate in.

To me, too many people have a warped sense of what ministry is. They think that the highest pinnacle of ministry is to be a pastor. If you have the title and the pulpit and the big office, then you must be just one step below

God Himself. But that's not right. Yes, Bible-preaching pastors who know how to shepherd their churches deserve respect and honor. It's grueling work if it's done right. But if you are called to be a children's Sunday school teacher, then when you're teaching those kids, God is smiling on you just as much as He's smiling on the guy who's preaching in the sanctuary. Or if your thing is directing traffic in the parking lot or running the sound for the service, He's just as proud of you if you're doing it with passion and excellence. When this life is over, there's not going to be a Beverly Hills section of heaven for all the pastors while everyone else has to live in spiritual skid row. Every servant of God who sacrifices their time and effort out of love will hear the words "Well done, good and faithful servant."

Ryan and I were doing a lot of events. If either Head or Lacey was available, they'd join in. Wherever we went, Ryan would promote The Whosoevers, and people were starting to connect with the concept of the movement. It's really so simple. We're just the nobodies of the world uniting. There's so much that divides the church. Imagine what we could do if we could get past the division and unite all the people of the church around the one primary and indisputable truth—salvation comes through faith in Jesus Christ alone. We could take over the world for God. I'm not talking in a militant way, but in a way where true, sacrificial love and unwavering hope and peace permeate every nation on earth.

Dude, it just hit me that my flower child mom would have been grinning from ear to ear if she had heard me say that.

The genesis of The Whosoevers as an event-based group took place in upstate New York. Ryan, Head, Lacey, and I, along with a good friend of ours, Melanie Savoie, had already spoken a handful of times in New York and Philadelphia due to a good friend of the Ries family named Pastor Nathan Robinson. He had set up for us to speak to different churches and groups and was so moved that he pretty much vouched for us to his pastor buddies throughout the northeast. Before you knew it, other pastors were wanting us to come through and speak to their churches.

Church speaking is cool and all, but we were hoping they'd be up for trying something a little different—an event for the community outside their stained-glass windowed walls. I knew a bunch of like-minded bands that were touring the area, so we hit them up to be a part. I also reached out to The Chariot down in Georgia, and they came up to play. What was cool was that we didn't have to work to convince any of the bands. The moment we'd explain The Whosoevers' mentality, they were like, "Love it, man! We're in!"

We stayed away from the blatantly Christian bands because our target was to reach the people outside of the church. The bands we brought in had an edge, but they believed in Jesus. They just weren't the ones who were out marketing Him for merch sales and concert attendance. And before I start getting huffy emails filling my inbox, I know there are a lot of great Christian groups doing it right and following the mission God has given them. But you and I both know that there are plenty of the other kind, and we could probably list them off together.

These bands we brought in were in the mix being excellent and gaining respect in the underground hardcore world. That kind of cred came because they were respecting their audience. The kids who came to their concerts didn't do it to get preached to. So the members of the band let their lives do the talking.

We were determined to bring that same level of respect to this New York crowd. We didn't want it to be the typical, "Oh, here comes the catch. Dude's going to get up now and tell us how we're all sinners." Instead, when Ryan and I stood up at the end, it was, "Hey, we love you guys. And we're going to be hanging out at this church tomorrow. Free coffee, free soda. We're thinking about getting a few pizzas. You see all these guys who just murdered this stage tonight? We're brothers and sisters. We all love Jesus, and we'd love to tell you about Him." Then we passed out flyers.

Of course, we didn't get the whole crowd there the next day. But the ones who came, they were the ones we could go deep with. They were the ones searching. Nobody could say, "Hey, they tricked me." They were there by choice, and they were ready to listen.

THAT WAS THE BEGINNING of what eventually morphed into what The Whosoevers is today, with Ryan going into schools and churches all over the world telling teens and adults about Jesus. Head, Lacey, and I join him when we can, but he's the one putting in the hard work, and God is using him. Thousands of people are getting saved through this movement every year. It's amazing.

But back in its origins, The Whosoevers was big events in addition to smaller meetings in group homes, youth detentions, jails, rehabs, churches—really, any place that would have us. We did pop-up, surprise concerts and skate contests and played wherever we could. We focused mainly on Southern California because it was the most cost efficient. But whenever we could raise the money or find financial support, we would jump into the van and drive across states. Head and Lacey were always ready to join us when their schedules allowed. We also recruited Ronnie Faisst from the Metal Mulisha, and he was ready to get down as well.

Not surprisingly, the Pharisees of the church took aim at the movement. "The Whosoevers are blasphemous! The Whosoevers are of the devil!" Head and I were used to the attacks, but I felt bad for Ryan. This was his first time experiencing the full force of these cynical, hypocritical keyboard warriors. It was brutal.

Time passed and we eventually came around to the second Exit concert. Head was there, along with The Chariot—all those groups again. The headlining band was P.O.D., which might give you a bit of a hint of the direction my search was leading me.

If I hadn't taken time away from the band, I can guarantee you that I would not be part of P.O.D. today. My year hiatus turned into almost three years, but I had no doubt that rock and roll was where God wanted me. The Sonny going back was very different than the one who needed to take a break. I had peace, I had purpose, and I had my tribe—a group of whosoevers just like me who were committed to living life in the mix so we could show our fellow nobodies of this world that life with Jesus is so much better than life without Him.

14

A LIGHTER LOAD

It's amazing what a little time away can do.

When I took a break from P.O.D., I was thinking that the band was probably done. I found myself wondering, "What next?" which was very strange to contemplate after so many years. But it was also kind of refreshing. It reminded me that I was not the band, and the band was not me. I had wrapped up all my mission in P.O.D. I felt that the band was my one opportunity to be a light. But I had lost focus, and as a result my light had gotten really dim.

Time away allowed me to think in silence without all the rock and roll noise around me. What was it I really wanted to accomplish with my life? Through that time of forming The Whosoevers, I had realized that my goal was for people to see Jesus the way I see Him. He's a guy who is not impressed with status or position. Religion is a waste of time to Him. What He wants is relationship.

Because of that, He spent so much of His time on earth going to those who were in desperate need of that connection. Even today, He's someone who loves the nobodies, the strugglers, the hurting, the outcasts. A heart searching for Him is more valuable than all the church buildings in the world. He has compassion on the broken and forgiveness for the rebels. Giving yourself to Him brings hope for the future, peace for today, and a deep, powerful joy that can somehow survive the worst this world has to bring.

Getting those who need Jesus most to understand that—that is my mission.

Those last four words clearly express another revelation I received during my hiatus. From the very beginning of P.O.D., I had been confusing my mission with the band's mission. Because I was called to this, we all must have been called to it. I don't blame myself. I was just a kid and a baby Christian. And I think in the early years, we all were on the same page. But we grew up and we each walked our own faith journeys.

It took me stepping away and viewing it from a distance to realize that truth. I found myself asking, "Man, why was I putting so much on the guys? Why was I expecting them to love the Lord the way I love the Lord?" Not that they didn't love Him. But expecting them to have the exact same relationship with God and carry the exact same calling? That kind of thinking is wrong and is begging for a fight. God walks with us individually. It wasn't my job to judge them or to fix them, if they even needed fixing. I had to trust that God had them in His control, and if He needed my help with anything, He'd be sure to hit me up.

LIKE I SAID, throughout the time off we still had commitments—fly outs to different gigs. About a year in, we had a short tour lined up for South America. This would be my first time heading overseas with this new individualized mission mindset. What I didn't know was that the reputation of The Whosoevers had already landed well before our plane. Right after arriving in Argentina, I had a guy come up and ask, "Sonny, you want to come over to our schools?" Somehow, word of mouth had spread that me and The Whosoevers were into hitting schools and rehabs and detention centers. Lucky for both this guy and me, the rumors weren't wrong. I was like, "Show me the way!" I think I did three different schools there.

The same thing happened a few months later when we did a fly out to Guatemala. As soon as I got off the plane, some pastors asked, "Sonny, do you want to come to the prisons with us?" I asked our tour manager, "Hey, we have time to do this?" He's like, "Uh, I guess so." Dude, let me just tell you right off, you do not want to be on the wrong side of the bars in a Guatemalan prison. But in between our P.O.D. shows, I had a chance to cut out and share the gospel with these prisoners. My cousin Wuv even came with me. It was nuts!

Back to the South America tour. Guido was with us, and he and I broke away one day. We were walking through a market, and he was asking me some probing questions, which is what he does best. Guido was one of the first people I had told about my vision for The Whosoevers, and he walked alongside me throughout that entire season. Now that P.O.D. was starting to play shows again, I still wasn't convinced that this was where God wanted me to be, or that *I* even wanted to be here. In actuality, I was looking for every reason not to go back to P.O.D., and I needed a little confirmation either way.

Suddenly, this guy comes running up to Guido and me. In broken English, he says, "Sonny from P.O.D.! I love Jesus! I love Jesus!" Then he starts telling me his whole life story, while Guido is sitting there grinning at me. A little later, we walked down an alley, and the same thing happened. In the middle of frickin' Brazil! I mean, we weren't even in a major city. We were in a quiet, sleepy town you could only find by taking a right at the third rubber tree past the river. These were just little confirmations of the impact that P.O.D. has had and of the calling that God had given me. It was our first time in South America, and we were learning again how God has loved on people, spoken to people, saved people all through P.O.D.'s music. And He had done it somehow without me, front man Sonny Sandoval, having had it all figured out.

There was one more confirmation that God gave me in Brazil. It was one of our first shows there. They speak Portuguese, so it's not like I could go up and start telling them about Jesus. God was going to have to do what He was going to do without me saying a thing. That realization was big for me.

For so long, I felt like the only way I could know for sure that the Holy Spirit was up there and moving was if I said something about God. In other words, God needed me to say something if He was going to accomplish something. That wasn't really a conscious thought. It was more of a mindset that came from my early days watching and learning mainstream Christianity. If you don't at least mention

Jesus dying on the cross for someone's sins, then what the hell are you doing up on the stage? Might as well just go and play your devil music and leave Jesus to the professionals.

Marcos was the one who helped set me straight on that. He used to ask me, "Why do you always feel like you have to say something?" Back then, I'd blow off the question. "That's just Marcos being Marcos." I didn't realize how much I'd been brainwashed into feeling like I had to prove myself to the Christian world. "See, we're doing the Lord's work. See, we're in God's will." As much as I told myself that I simply needed to be myself onstage, I still found that I was feeling like I had to prove my calling to that one self-righteous Christian in the audience who came only so they could later post, "See, P.O.D. didn't say nothing about Jesus. They didn't even pray! Hypocrites!"

After the time off, I realized just how right Marcos was about a lot of stuff. God doesn't need my voice for Him to speak. I'm a musician. He's called me to speak through my music and my life. I'll save my words for backstage or after the show or when someone from another band says, "Dude, I've got to talk to someone."

So, I went on the stage that night in Brazil, and we were killing it. Even as we were playing, I'm thinking, *Holy Spirit, I need you to show up tonight.* I can't remember what song we were doing when I jumped up on the barricade. Then I fell.

Dude, I jacked myself up. I'm reaching out, trying to pull myself back up. Suddenly, I felt all these hands on me—people reaching out from all around. A lot of times during concerts, I find myself praying for people I see. But this time, I felt them praying for me. In that moment, I felt the Holy Spirit strengthening me, empowering me to get back onstage and finish the set. My prayer had been that the Holy Spirit show up in the audience. Instead, He showed up in me.

But the story's not over. After we got back home, I got an email from a Brazilian guy. He's like, "I don't believe in God, but I've always loved P.O.D. I was at that show when you fell off the barricade. I watched when you were trying to get back up. All those people were hugging you and you were hugging them. I think you were praying for them, and they were praying for you. If that's God and His spirit, I want that. I need that."

I responded and told him my whole story. I wrote, "Thank you. Whether you know it or not, God just used you to speak into my life and confirm once again that He is real. And wasn't it cool how God let you know how special you are to Him that He was willing to split the sky and come down to some rock concert just so He could show you how much He loves you?" That began a friendship that has lasted over the years, just short, encouraging emails sent back and forth every now and then.

MOST OF 2010 WAS SPENT getting our feet wet again. We were still doing a lot of these one-offs, like that Guatemala trip and joining Korn for a show in Costa Rica. We hadn't committed to any tours, and I was hesitant to go all in. But after all the amazing things God was doing with The Whosoevers and my renewed desire to share my faith,

I decided to give it another shot. So, at one point I said to the guys, "You ready to do another record or what?" They're like, "You serious? Finally!"

We started writing. Same process as before—record a couple tunes, get things going. At the time, there was a studio over in Escondido where I think Traa was doing some stuff. We booked some time and recorded a few demos.

One of the first songs we did was called "I Am." The tune is driving, it's mean. When I was writing the lyrics, my mind went into the dark places the music created. I sing about murderers, perverts, drug users, prostitutes, sexual abuse victims, and sexual abusers.

These are the voices of the sinners, the victims, the perpetrators. These are the violent, the battered, the hopeless. They are the nobodies and the rejected that our society turns its back on.

The chorus then takes the listener to the moment that each of these people is confronted with the truth that Jesus died on the cross for them. But they find the concept unbelievable, inconceivable. They know who they are and what they've done. Yet, they hear that there is Someone who can see beyond their current life to what they can become. There is Someone who still holds out hope for them, who believes in them.

While it's true that "I Am" ran into some serious controversy because of some of the lyrics, there is no other song I have written that's given me the same "changed life" feedback. It wasn't long before I started hearing stories on the road or from social media of people saying, "Dude, I heard that song and I fell on my face and gave my life to the Lord." One story I heard was of a cop, coldest and most ruthless on the force, who had gone from Iraq straight to the streets of Philly. Another cop buddy of his said, "Dude, I want you to listen to this song." By the end, the first cop was in tears, giving his life to the Lord. People were looking for real, and that's what our album *Murdered Love* gave to them.

BEFORE I GET TO THE RELEASE of *Murdered Love*, I realize I still have a loose end hanging out there with INO/Columbia. If there was one group that really got screwed by P.O.D.'s breakup, it was our label. They had no idea that all this drama was going to happen. When we decided to take a year off, all they could say was, "Uh, okay . . ."

It really left a sour taste in their mouth. The owner of INO, Jeff Moseley, is a believer, which is one of the reasons we went with them. They had done some things with Flyleaf and had a good reputation. When we didn't fulfill our duties, I'm sure they lost financially. Once I started getting myself figured out, I tried reaching out to Jeff. I remember thinking that it was the honorable, godly thing to do. But what it really came down to was that I really felt bad about how things ended, and I wanted to make it right. I thought maybe if I could explain to him all that was going on, we might be able to figure out a way to make it up. I never heard back from him.

I went back to Israel in 2011, and this time I took my wife. It was awesome seeing her face every time she saw something new and connected it with the Bible. One night in Tiberias, along the shores of the Sea of Galilee, we were hanging out on the back patio of our hotel. Out of the blue, this older, sophisticated white lady walked up to me and said, "Sonny?" I'm looking at her thinking, *This lady is definitely not a P.O.D. Warrior.*

"You're Sonny with P.O.D., right?"

"Uh, yeah," I answered.

"I'm Jeff Moseley's wife."

I was floored. "Hey, can we please talk after dinner?" I asked.

That evening overlooking the beautiful biblical lake, I got to explain the whole thing to her. This is what I was going through. This is where I am now. Dude, she was the sweetest, most understanding person. I told her, "Please, I've been trying to get hold of your husband. I would love to just thank him and speak to him, if possible." She couldn't promise anything, but she said she'd let him know.

I never did end up talking with Jeff. That's cool. I get it. But we did hear from INO that they were dropping all the money that we still owed them for not fulfilling the contract. Not only that, but they gave us our masters for *When Angels & Serpents Dance.* The album belonged to us now to do with what we wanted. That's how we were able to rerelease the album in 2022. One day we were like, "Why are we just sitting on this album? Everyone keeps asking about it. Let's get it out."

Of all places to get the reconciliation process rolling, halfway across the world along the shores of the Sea of Galilee. Just another one of those coincidences, right? Even though I haven't spoken to Jeff, I believe God has reconciled his heart. I know that He did mine. What was especially cool was to come to my guys and say, "Guess who I ran into?" Then when he cleared our name? It's just an incredible story. Little reminders that God is always watching out for us.

"LOST IN FOREVER" was our first single off *Murdered Love*, and it hit number one on the rock charts. We shot a great video for our second single, "Higher," then that same night we decided to knock out another video—this one for the title track. Even though it was never going to be a single, we really wanted to get "Murdered Love" out there. Marcos's staticky guitar riff and my off-cadence rap combined with an epic vocal from Sick Jacken from Psycho Realm to create one of my favorite songs we've done. Sick Jacken wasn't our only guest appearance on the record. Sen Dog of Cypress Hill and Hatebreed's Jamey Jasta dropped in as nods to both our hip hop and our old-school metalcore fans.

Razor & Tie gave some push to the album, and "Higher" charted at least in the top ten. We hit the road to support *Murdered Love* and toured our butts off. But this tour was different than any I had done in the past. I mentioned a few chapters ago that I had brought my five-year-old son, Justice, on a tour with me. This was that time, and it was beautiful. I've always known how important it is for a son to have a father. Having Justice with me taught me how much a father can learn from having a son.

My boy helped me focus on what was most important. Watching him reminded me to concentrate on the joy of the moment. Screw the ministry agenda, screw the business end, screw the obligations of being "band leader"—a title that I probably only held in my own mixed-up mind. I was going to enjoy every second with my son, every second with my band, every second onstage. And seeing Justice's simple love for God reminded me of what my "first love" experience was like out in that hospital parking lot while my mom was inside dying.

It wasn't just simple love that he showed me, but simple faith. Seeing my son holding hands with me and some hardcore rocker from another band or a struggling fan who caught up with me after the show, and hearing Justice pray for that person knowing beyond a shadow of a doubt that God would answer because that's just what God does—dude, that is purity. That is the perfect faith of a child that Jesus talked about. An experience like that will clear all the ritualistic religion and unbiblical legalism and false personal expectations out of your heart and mind, leaving you with nothing but the perfect foundation of Christianity—love God and love others.

Yeah, my son taught me that. Not bad for a five-year-old.

Having Justice along didn't just make an impact on me. So many times, the crew guys or the band guys or friends from other bands and crews would say, "Dude, I just love watching you with your son," or "Thanks for sharing your son with us." For a lot of them, I think it may have been the first time they had seen the way a father and son relationship should be—not that I had it perfect, by any means.

Even today, when my son goes to a show with me, he'll see people and they'll say, "Dang, dude, you've gotten so big!" But that's kind of the rock and roll world. We all share each other's lives. People focus so much on the sex and drugs part of rock and roll, but there are great parts to it too. For a lot of us, we're all part of a weird and wild family, and like most families, you just do life together.

WE DID A LOT OF COOL SHOWS before and after the release of *Murdered Love*. In August and September 2011, we did the Rock Allegiance tour, then the next fall we slotted into the Uproar tour. But even before those, in the summer, we headlined a tour alongside Red. Head joined us with his band, Love and Death, and a lot of times he would crash in the back of the bus with Justice and me, sometimes bringing his teenage daughter, Jennea.

At the beginning of May, Red and P.O.D. split off the tour for a night, playing the Carolina Rebellion in Rockingham. Korn was headlining, along with Shinedown, Evanescence, and Staind. Head asked if he and Jennea could tag along. He was hoping to team up with his old bandmates and somehow make amends. When we got there, we had to sound check. Head told me that while we did that, he was going to go track down the guys.

By this time, he had already reached out to Fieldy, and things were good between them, partly because Fieldy had given his life to the Lord too. It was okay with Jonathan, but he was still very hurt from Head leaving the band. But Head still hadn't reached out to Munky because he figured that dude was just waiting to rip him a new one. I had been bugging him to hit up the guys, so when he said he was heading over to them, I was psyched. You could see his nerves, so Justice and I prayed for him and Jennea, and off they went.

When they came back, Head had a big smile on his face. But I could tell he was still nervous about something. He said, "Everything was great with them. And, Sonny, they asked me if I wanted to play the last song with them." God answers prayer, my friend. I told him, "Dude, you got this!"

We did our set, then I came back to the bus to do some interviews. Justice was back with me doing his thing. By that time, the rear of the bus looked like a schoolroom with worksheets and maps and pictures he had colored all over the walls. Not quite what you expect when you go to the back of a rock and roll tour bus. Once Korn started playing, I told the interviewer, "I may have to bolt out of here." I didn't tell him why, because at that time the only ones who knew about the secret guest appearance were Korn, P.O.D., and Head.

Then I heard that iconic hi-hat kick introing their classic song "Blind." The guitar riff started, and I said to the interviewer, "Sorry, man, gotta go!" I grabbed Justice, and we ran toward the side of the stage. The security guard tried to step in my way, and I held up my laminate and pushed past him. We made it to the side of the stage, and what I saw was magic to any Korn fan. But to me, it was spiritual. I had been walking with Head through his journey. I knew the backstory.

They played the song. Head was doing his thing. The crowd was going absolutely nuts. Then, when the song ended, Jonathan walked up to Head and wrapped him up in a huge hug. When they separated, Jonathan started to say something, but he couldn't because he was bawling his eyes out. I was thinking, *I don't know if anyone else saw it, but I just witnessed God moving.*

Jonathan finally regained his composure and said the band's goodbyes to the audience. "God bless you! Good night, people! We love you!" Dude, this was JDevil talking. He never said, "God bless you!" It was a crazy night.

When Head got back on the bus, he was shaking. It was just me, Head, Jennea, and Justice. For so long he had said that he was never going back to Korn. It was part of his story every time he talked. "I gave up so many millions of dollars, but it was the best decision of my life"—stuff like that.

One day when he had repeated to me how he's never going back to Korn, I said, "Really, dude? Because I've actually been praying just the opposite." He wasn't expecting that. I'm like, "Yeah, man, I've been praying that when the time is right, you do go back to Korn. Bro, you have to stop being afraid of your own shadow. Are you going to just keep on speaking at churches?"

God had given him talent, a history, crazy experiences, and a beautiful story of redemption. He's a walking example of, "If this dude can get his life straightened out, then I sure as hell can too." To paraphrase Jesus, I essentially told Head, "What are you doing spending all your time talking to the healthy when it's the sick who need a doctor?" But for him, not only was the church safer, at least somewhat, but he didn't figure Korn would ever want him back. I told him, "Dude, these are your brothers, and they're just hurt. Apologize to them. Not because you necessarily did anything wrong, but just to let them

240

know your heart and that the last thing you ever meant to do was hurt them."

After the concert, Head was able to hang out a little bit more with the guys. When he came back later, he said, "Dude, it's all cool. Munky was cool. It's all smiles. It's all love." Not much longer after that they asked him to come back to the band.

As if I needed one more reason for the church to hate me.

There was an interview Head did after rejoining Korn. By that time, he was so sick of explaining his reason for going back to the band that he simply told this interviewer, "Oh, just blame it on Sonny from P.O.D. It's his fault." The guy wrote that in his article, and suddenly my phone is blowing up with DMs and emails screaming at me and calling me the devil. Damn, how the church loves to eat its own.

We toured our butts off through 2012 and into 2013. It was still tense at times within the band. I think that we were so worried about offending one another that we weren't being real anymore. I found myself retreating more and more to the back of the bus, using Justice as an excuse to isolate. We were together, but the band wasn't healthy. Then, rock and roll started prowling for another victim, and this time her eyes were on us.

15

FULL CIRCLE

Grinding.

My whole life has been grinding. As a teenager I got that job at the grocery store because I wanted my independence. I didn't care if I had to work nights while all my buddies were out partying and having a good time. There's nothing worth having that doesn't take work to get. If my guys and I were going to be a successful band, we knew from the jump that it meant playing show after show, hitting the road so that we were with each other far more than we were home with our families.

It's just, I kind of thought there was going to come a time when I would be able to slow down and enjoy home more. Making my money from rock and roll, I figured that eventually I'd have enough in the bank that the hard grind might smooth out a bit. Dude, that's never happened.

And it never will. The money will never be the same as it was during *Fundamental* and *Satellite*. But it's not just the money that keeps weighing on me and pushing me down. It's all the bumps and bruises with labels and business and dramas in the extended family and the never-ending suck of being caught in the vortex between rock and roll and the church.

I know some may be out there saying, "Cry me a frickin' river, Sonny. You should see my life." Dude, I know it. I'm not complaining. I'm just saying that the rock and roll lifestyle that most people think about only belongs to a handful of people. Most of us are like everyone else in the world; you keep slogging until your body gives out and you can't slog anymore. I've been blessed that my slog includes doing something that I love and that lets me visit amazing places around the world.

Again, no complaints here. I guess it comes down to the fact that what most people think about the realities of the rock and roll life, they've read it in a book or watched on *MTV Cribs*. I learned the hard way, from a label shafting us when we were on top to my CPA telling me, "Bro, you got a family to feed. You better get your butt back out on the road." Rock and roll is a grind.

So, that's exactly what we did.

THE BAND HIT SHOW AFTER SHOW. We'd get back on the bus, sleep for three hours, then turn up at a radio station to play a song or two. It was like we were a new band again, back to the days of *Fundamental* with all the interviews and radio giveaways and DJs. "Hey, come have pizza with P.O.D.!" "Hey, come bowl with P.O.D.!" Even when we were on the big tours, it was the same. Like with Uproar, we headlined the side stage in the late afternoon. After our set, there were many days we'd leave right away to go play an acoustic gig at some cool spot or as a reward for the winners of a radio contest. Again, always hustling.

That first tour with Justice tagging along went so well that he stayed out with me on the road. From the time he was five until he was nine, just about every time I left home, my little dude was with me. I loved it. Justice was my outlet to fade away from all the craziness and drama that was around me. He gave me a purpose beyond the "lather, rinse, repeat" of sound check, interviews, play the show, leave for the next city. During the festivals, especially, when we'd typically be on in the afternoon, I couldn't wait to finish our set, shower up, and then take him to catering. We'd set up a miniclassroom to do his schoolwork, or if he was caught up, we'd just people watch.

It was an adjustment, of course, when he first came on our headlining tours. The band wouldn't take the stage until ten or eleven at night. We had to rework his whole sleep and schoolwork schedule. But he was a kid and he adapted right away.

When he was super young, I'd always give him a red cup of M&M's or something before we went on, just to give him a bit of sugar. But once he had his big, old earmuffs on, it wouldn't be long until he'd start nodding off. Our drum tech, Mike Kelley, would usually see when he was about to fall asleep onstage. He'd hustle over and snatch him up, then lay him behind Wuv. When this turned into a regular thing,

Mike went to Walmart and got the biggest dog bed he could find. Before the show, whether it was a rock club or theater or arena, he'd set it up behind the drum set. When Justice started to doze, he'd carry him onstage behind the drums and lay him down in the dog bed. People in the audience would be like, "What the heck just happened?"

As he grew older, Justice became part of the rock and roll family. The crews and the members of the other bands all got to know him, and they always tried to mind their p's and q's around him. One day, one of the rock stars said something a kid has no business hearing. When he saw Justice, he was like, "Ah, man. Sorry. Here's a buck, dude." From that moment, it just became a thing. Every time someone swore, they'd drop him some cash. He would come home at the end of every tour with hundreds of dollars in his swear jar.

Build-A-Bear was a big thing back then, and Justice was still young enough to be into it. Word got around, and soon his bunk was filled with stuffed animals. He'd leave the tours having to somehow get thirty Build-A-Bears back home. I told him, "Dude, we can't do this. We don't have the room!"

People think that rock and roll tours are nothing but drinking and debauchery. They're not. It's a community, a family. Twisted and weird at times, sure. But rock and roll is just a bunch of people living their lives, earning a living, and doing it together.

SOMEWHERE ALONG THE LINE, we ended our business relationship with Tim Cook. He had done a lot for us through the years, but it was time. We toyed with a few different managers but then found our way back to Angelica Cob, now Angelica Cob-Baehler. Geli, as we knew her, was part of our Atlantic family way back when and now was getting back into management as part of a group called The Firm. She was amazing. We loved her, her husband, and her family. When she tragically passed away of cancer in 2018, it left a void in our hearts and in the music industry. Geli, we love you and miss you dearly.

Now that we had our new manager, we also needed a new label. We dug around and ended up going with T-Boy. Geli and The Firm brought us the deal, and T-Boy seemed legit because they had signed Eagles of Death Metal and Megadeth. We connected back up with Howard Benson and began working on *The Awakening*.

Marcos had an idea for the new record. He's an old-school metalhead, and he remembered the great concept albums of bands like Pink Floyd, Queensrÿche, and Iron Maiden. He said, "We should do a concept record. No one's done a concept record in decades." We thought, "Cool. Why not?"

We dove deep into *The Awakening*! There was a story-line laid out for the album, and we had a vision for shooting a video for each song then combining those videos into a short story movie. It was probably about as much fun as we've had laying out an album's concept. Once we were done, we were ready for *The Awakening* to shake up the rock world!

Then T-Boy screwed us over. I don't want to get into details, because the dude who ran T-Boy is just the kind of joker who would drop a lawsuit just to bleed us dry. Not that I need to worry about him showing up. In the fifteen years since he left our album hanging, I haven't seen him or heard of him. That's probably for the better. The guys and I have discussed what we might do if we ever did see him again, and it's just possible that a slight amount of violence might be involved. Actually, what's really aggravating is knowing that if I ever did see the dude, the Holy Spirit in me would probably force me to go up to him and hug it out. That would suck!

The Awakening never really saw the light of day. So, we were back to hustling just to survive. In hindsight, I now know why Geli wasn't as active during that record. She was silently preoccupied with her health. We did put together a video for "This Goes Out to You," but that was just us using one of our homies, shooting out on the road. It was a cool video, but it wouldn't have happened if we didn't make it happen. There were no singles released to radio, no other videos, nothing. Just more of the same tours and shows leaving us grinding like always to pay the bills.

AFTER THE HARSH BLOW of *Awakening*, the band slowly began to dismantle once again. We could all feel it. Wuv was doing his thing. Traa was in the process of moving to Nashville. This was another of those juncture moments when the future of P.O.D. could go either way. In the past, writing had always been our answer to the big blows. So, what do you do? You get everyone together to write a new album. That, however, was much easier said than done.

We recruited HEAVY, a production team made up of Jordan Miller and Jason Bell, who were a fresh, young production duo making noise in the alternative and pop world. While we were constantly struggling to get all four of us in the studio at the same time, these guys stepped in and helped to keep things fresh with their outside perspective. They treaded lightly with their input, excelling at moving things around, adding in loops and sounds, suggesting a little bit here and a little bit there.

Writing and recording *Circles* felt like an eternity. There were so many obstacles in the way that I didn't think we'd ever get through it. When it was finally done, we had a unique record with more of an alternative feel. There were heavy tracks in there, but there were some poppy and fun moments also.

Jumping ahead, writing our latest album, *Veritas*, mirrored *Circles* in a lot of ways. We were reeling during the COVID years. It seemed other bands were writing records to get through the time, but we were too wrapped up in band and financial dramas. Finally, the label told us, "You guys need to write a record." Marcos and I were like, "How are we going to do that? We don't have Traa or Wuv, and California is shut tight."

We knew we wanted to use HEAVY again, and this was definitely the best scenario for trying to write some new tunes. Marcos and I would make a day trip up to Hollywood whenever the guys were free and start laying down ideas that would eventually become *Veritas*. I don't know if it was our post-COVID mood or that we just wanted to get back to our roots, but this album ended up much heavier than *Circles*. I know I say the same thing about every new album, but it's quite possible that *Veritas* is my favorite record we've ever done.

Putting together *Veritas* was unlike any other record. Marcos would lay down one of his killer riffs, then HEAVY could build the drums right there on their computer. They'd add in some loops, and all of a sudden we've got a makeshift beat that would carry us through the songwriting process. Later, we'd add in real drums, even though fake drums have gotten so good now that a lot of these newer bands don't even bother. Just more of AI taking over the world.

WE HAD SIGNED WITH MASCOT, an international label group based in Rotterdam, Netherlands. They have an eclectic stable of artists and carry a very strong overseas presence; both were reasons we were drawn to them. No surprise to us, when *Circles* dropped in November 2018, it hit big across the ocean. We took off to where the greatest interest was with nearly two months' worth of touring in Europe. We hit all the major military bases in Germany and the UK, along with theaters and clubs throughout the continent. It was a huge start for us.

Because Wuv couldn't join us overseas, our drum tech, Jonny Beats, filled in for him. He had been with us for years, so he killed all the songs. We brought along Alien Ant Farm and '68 on this first leg, and it was so successful that we got called out later in the year for a second leg. When we went back to Europe, Dead Girls Academy joined us and Alien Ant Farm. From the end of October through the month of November, we hit eighteen countries, some of them places we had never been before. At least sixteen years had passed since we had headlined a tour in Europe, so the response on both legs blew us away. It was a beautiful thing.

Shannon had come out with Justice for some shows on the first leg of our European tour. When she left from London, Justice stayed. I knew the schedule we had ahead and all the places we would be. This was too good an opportunity for him to miss. At first his school was hesitant, but we finally worked it out for him to write each day about all the places he'd been and what he'd seen.

Justice had gone out with me on summer gigs and one-offs, but now for the first time after a handful of years, he was back on the road. We did a lot in the UK. Then we hit Belgium and Denmark. We did three shows in Ireland and Scotland. It was epic! Problem was that the road and the weather were catching up to me. It gets freaking cold and wet in Europe in March! I felt myself getting sick, and each night I wondered if that was the show when my voice would go. Amazingly, though, through the whole tour, God gave me just enough for the show, even when I was on antibiotics and feeling like crap.

But even though I was sick as a dog, I refused to let Justice miss anything from the places we went to. All those sights and activities you read about in books, from taking the ferry cruise ships over the English Channel and the Irish Sea to seeing the massive White Cliffs of Dover to walking through most of the major cities in the UK to relaxing in an Irish pub in Limerick eating lamb stew, I made sure my son experienced it all.

When the tour with Alien Ant Farm and '68 ended, P.O.D. still had some shows left. We flew to Ukraine and did a couple performances in Kyiv and Lviv. Years later, when Russia invaded Ukraine, Justice was glued to the news reports. He was looking up things and asking questions. "Hey, that's where Johnny got pickpocketed on the train, right?" "Yeah, Justice, that's Kyiv."

From there we went to St. Petersburg. When you do Russia, usually you do St. Petersburg one night and Moscow the next. Whichever order you book them, there is typically a twelve-hour train ride from one city to the other. The train is the kind you see in movies, with the bunk beds and the dining cars. It's an amazing experience. We even had three young, drunk Russian travelers stumble into our cabin. Traa, Justice, and I had a lovely chat with them for hours.

When we arrived in Russia, we learned the airlines had lost all of our equipment and all of our clothes. The only things that came in were the guitars and the bass. But that's all we needed. We makeshifted the whole show. We raided the merch for shirts, cobbled together a few different effect pedals from the stagehands, and we murdered the show. But by the time we got back to the hotel, all I wanted to do was crash. We had an early flight to the Faroe Islands where we'd end the tour. I put in a quick call to my wife.

"Hey, we just got back to the hotel."

"Have you taken Justice to Red Square?" she asked.

"Nah, it's just so late and we're exhausted. Besides, we have no clothes."

She's like, "Sonny, you need to take your son to see Red Square."

What was I going to say? She was dead right. Even though it was already 1:30 in the morning, I somehow tracked down a Russian Uber-ish ride. I hit up Jonny Beats to join us, and he was all in. So, we took off to Red Square with my boy. It took an hour and a half to get there, and we only stayed about fifteen minutes, but it was so cool. By that time, it was like 3:30 in the morning and nobody was around. But it was still lit up, and it was beautiful. I wouldn't trade that experience with my son for the world.

THE YEAR 2019 WAS AMAZING for the band financially. We worked our butts off the entire twelve months, finishing off with a New Year's Eve show in El Paso. The next year, 2020, looked like it would be just as good. We already had summer tours lined up in Europe along with shows throughout the US. It finally seemed like we were getting our legs under us again. I was able to pay off debts from the lean years, and 2020 was going to finally put me ahead again.

Then we start hearing rumors about this virus that was going around. Scratch the European tours. Scratch the American dates. Scratch everything. Suddenly, all that money that I had made in 2019 was being stretched to try to survive 2020. Rock and roll for us is like everything else; if you don't work, you don't eat. There are only so many artists who live that luxurious life of checks coming in all the time until you die, and that ain't us. I was looking at my bank account, thinking, *I've got one kid in college, two others in sports, and a family to feed.* Thankfully, I get free clothes from the coolest brands out. Can't remember the last time I had to buy a shirt. Chalk one up for rock and roll!

Like I said earlier, it was a tough time for a lot of reasons. When it comes down to it, the easiest problems to work through were the financial ones. But through it all, I never once doubted that God would take care of us. We can't let our tough times define who we think God is. My life sucks, so God either hates me, doesn't give a crap about me, or doesn't exist. That is dead-end thinking. We've got to turn that around and see that it is not God who is messed up, but it's this world that sucks. For now, He's allowing that suck to continue, but there will come a day when He's going to clean it all up. In the meantime, He is there to carry us through the bad times. In Him, we can find hope and peace that will get us through each day.

I'll admit that there are times when I get angry with God. I ask Him why, when I'm trying as hard as I can to do the right thing, I still face all these troubled times, whether it's label stupidity or financial struggles or family drama or whatever. And what I've found is that God has big shoulders. He can handle me venting at Him. He doesn't get angry when I speak my mind to Him. Take a look at the Psalms in the Bible. They're full of King David asking God why He's holding back His blessing. But what David knew and what I know and what I want you to know is that when you're through pouring out your heart to Him, He'll still be there with His arms open, wanting you to feel and experience His deep love for you.

I WANT TO WRAP THIS UP by going back to the Faroe Islands. Again, I was sick and on antibiotics. Every day I was saying, "Lord, just get me through the next show." Most days, I was barely talking just to keep my voice. That night, we killed the set. Great audience, totally into it. We had met a bunch of new friends—promoters who had come out—and we wanted to hang around and talk, but it was late and it was the last show of the tour. Our crew and everyone else had just enough energy to get back to the hotel, get something to eat, and crash.

But when we got to the hotel, we discovered they had no food. Beautiful.

Then someone said, "There's an old pizza spot right around the way." We had to eat, so out into the gusting wind we went. The Faroe Islands is like no other place I've been. It has a *Truman Show* vibe where everything seems fake, like it's staged and there are cameras following you around. It's beautiful, incredibly friendly, with just a slight tinge of creepy. But I'd go back in a heartbeat.

We got our pizza, and as we were walking back, we heard music. Not far from us we saw a three-story building that looked like it was a frat house that someone turned into a club. The tunes had us all bobbing our heads, so we decided to check it out. We looked for the bouncer and spotted this petite little lady. She greets us with, "You guys did such a great show!" I pointed to Justice and asked, "Can he get in?" She looked skeptically and answered, "Hmmm, how old is he?" Then she laughed and said to him, "Go ahead." There are definitely different bar rules in Europe. Just a few weeks prior in Antwerp, Belgium, I was with Shannon and Justice. Walking past an Irish pub, we saw all my guys and the Alien Ant Farm boys. We asked if Justice could go in, and the bartender pointed at my boy and said, "Yeah, but no whiskey for him."

Back in the Faroe Islands, the bottom floor of the club was like a beer garden with everyone drinking their pints and smoking cigarettes. We continued upstairs to where the music was. Again, it had a frat house feel with a DJ up front and everyone on the floor dancing. The guys grabbed drinks and headed to the dance floor. Justice and I hung out on the outside watching everybody have a good time. All the while I was thinking, *Shannon is going to kill me for bringing him to this place.* Actually, if I'm totally honest, Shannon would have dragged me and Justice onto the dance floor, and together we would have shown our new Faroese friends how to get down Southtown style!

So, we were hanging out when some dude came up and said, "Man, great show!" He went on for a bit, then disappeared. A few minutes later he came back with a beer for me and a ginger beer for Justice. It was a crazy scene. Justice and I were laughing because they were playing Biggie Smalls and all kinds of other music you just don't expect to hear on this little Danish island halfway between Norway and Iceland.

I remember looking at my son and realizing that it was all about to come to an end. We were ready to head home, and all I had left was this moment with him. All the emotions I had in me swirled together with my tiredness and my sickness. My mind was racing, thinking, *This is a story he's going to tell his grandkids someday about being here with his dad in this frat house, him sipping on his ginger beer while his dad drank from his mug, and all the guys were out dancing and having fun while we were chilling, having just had the experience of a lifetime . . .*

I reached over and grabbed Justice by the shoulders. Looking him square in the eyes, I said, "Live your life! Live your life!" And when I said it, my emphasis was on the second word of that sentence.

God created my son as a unique person with a unique purpose. He has given him experiences that no other kid gets to have. Through those years on the road, he had a chance to learn that being a Christian isn't just about talking about Jesus or following rules. It's about loving people. It's about sacrificing for them. It's about living the life that God gave to you and being the person that God created you to be.

For too many kids, all they see of Christianity is that hour or two on Sunday morning when Mom and Dad drag them to church. Then for the rest of the week, there is no encounter with the God of the universe. There's no experience of His daily loving-kindness and grace. There's no freedom. That's not true Christianity. That's religion. That's simply going through their spiritual routines. For them, church becomes just a scheduled time in their calendars to go and get their God fix.

If you want to see God, then you need to look in the spontaneous moments when God pushes you to act, and you follow through. It's in the risks and the sacrifices that you see and feel His love. That's when God gets real. Justice met the real God on the day it was cold and we brought food to a guy outside the show, then gave him my jacket and scarf and beanie. "Here, sir, take this. It's cold outside." He met the real God when we woke up and saw the homeless guy passed out from drugs, so we quickly made peanut butter and jelly sandwiches and set them next to him. That guy's never going to know who did that. But for us to be able to give that to him and pray over him, that's where my son saw the real Jesus.

One night while Justice was watching, the guys in the band were all signing autographs along a fence. Suddenly, this mom came running to us, screaming and screaming. I let her through, and she bawled as she embraced me. She began telling me how her daughter was cutting herself and was determined to kill herself. But then her girl heard "Beautiful" on the radio—that's why they came to the show. She begged me to meet her daughter.

Her daughter slowly walked in, embarrassed and ashamed. I could see that my son was watching the whole episode. She came up, and the first thing I did was lift her jacket sleeves, and she was cut from her elbow down to her wrists. I said, "Baby girl, what are you doing? Don't you know that God loves you so much and this just breaks His heart? His heart is broken that you're so sad. Promise me that you'll never do this again."

All around us, people were watching. No one cared about their autographs anymore. Instead, they were looking at us as we're crying and praying. I prayed over her, and Justice came in and laid his hands on her. So many people on the other side of the fence were joining us, praying for her.

That moment—it was just so Jesus. Nothing else compares.

Live *your* life. That is my message to you. Don't let anyone force you into a mold or a box. Remember, Jesus gave His life so that whosoever believes in Him will have eternal life. There is no qualification to that. He'll take you exactly how you are right this very moment. If you genuinely give yourself heart, mind, and soul to Him, He'll take care of the rough edges in His time and in His way. You don't need to get yourself straight before you come to Him; He'll help get you straight after you come to Him. Just ask my boys, Head and Ryan.

Then get yourself a Bible and start reading it. Find yourself a church that preaches what Jesus said, not what their traditions demand. The more you get into the real Jesus, the more you'll find Someone who cares much more about what's inside of you than what you look like on the outside.

God has given me a life I could never have dreamed of. I have been places I couldn't have imagined ever going, and I have met people that others would kill to meet. I have been truly blessed.

But it hasn't been smooth as I've tried to remain true to myself through it all. What I can tell you unequivocally is that life with Jesus is so much better than life without Him. I have seen people on both sides of that coin at their highest highs and at their lowest lows. It's only with Jesus that those at their highest highs find satisfaction and those at their lowest lows find peace.

Live your life, my friend. But don't do it alone. Bring along the One who will never let you down and who will never leave your side.

EPILOGUE

It was Thanksgiving Day, 2018. The guys and I were doing a quick tour with Nonpoint right before we headed back to Europe. Somewhere in the vastness of Texas, east of El Paso, we became stranded. Not stranded in the sense of our buses broke down. We were stranded by the regulations of the bus drivers' union that states any miles driven over the five-hundred-mile limit require overdrive payment. Forget that. We were in the middle of nowhere and there were no major cities en route, so we pulled off onto an overpass somewhere just to the right of nowhere.

This was the kind of unsettling place they make movies about. There was a gas station, a 99-cent store, and an old, abandoned motel. The whole thing was creepy. The motel's pool had been filled in with dirt, begging the question, "How many of the former guests are buried in the deep end?" But we figured it was reasonably safe to post up there so the drivers could rest.

Being away from home on holidays is always tough, and missing that Thanksgiving was hitting us all pretty hard.

But we decided to make the best of it. We walked over to the store and raided their microwavable foods and chips. Someone snagged some deli meats and some sausages, and we stocked up on drinks.

When we got back to the buses, we lit up a fire and turned on some music. Food was getting passed around, and a few of the gang were trying to barbecue the little sausages over the firepit. We were doing everything we could to make this Thanksgiving away from home suck a little less. Unfortunately, it wasn't really working.

But then Elias Soriano, lead singer for Nonpoint, spoke up. "One thing I love about my rock and roll family. We pass each other through the years. We don't always have time to hang out and catch up. What I love is that when we are together, we just pick up right where we left off."

Isn't that what family really is? Life often takes you different directions, but when you're back together, you find you haven't lost anything. The love still exists. The history and shared experiences haven't changed. There's a genuine excitement about seeing each other.

No doubt, if I had been given the opportunity to spend that Thanksgiving at home with my wife and kids, carving the turkey, mashing the potatoes, serving up the pies, I would've taken it in a heartbeat. But there in the middle of nowhere, hanging with my rock and roll family—yeah, not a bad day after all.

OVER THE YEARS, I've spent plenty of time complaining about going out on the road. I'm a homebody. There's no place

I'd rather be than with my wife and kids. But when COVID came along and that "road" part of my life was taken away, I realized just how much I missed it. Sure, being away is hard, but there is something incredibly special about being able to travel the world making music with my guys. Every festival we hit, every venue we play, I get to reunite with the friends and family I've made over the decades. Even as I'm writing this epilogue, we've just announced a major tour schedule to support *Veritas*, and I am stoked to get back on the road. Truly, I am blessed beyond measure.

But if I'm totally honest, part of the reason I'm anxious to get on tour is because there have been some difficult times in my family. Shannon and I and the kids, we're all good. But during the writing of this book, my Noni passed away. She was our matriarch, the hub that held all the spokes in place. Without her strength and stability, a lot of old issues within the extended family were stirred up. But even beyond that, I'm just struggling to get used to a Noni-less life. She was there for me from the day I was born, and when my mom passed, she took an even more important place in my life. But now that she's gone? It's tough, man. This one's going to take a while. What makes the pain even greater is that it's been more than just my Noni. I've had more friends and family pass away in the past few years than ever before.

I DIDN'T SET OUT to write a how-to book on life, and I hope it hasn't come across that way. My hope was just to show you how one guy has done it. What was my "secret sauce" for life? It's not that complicated. It's really just loving God, trusting Him, and moving on day by day. As imperfectly as I've walked that mantra, I think it's worked out okay.

Outside of the band, one of the ways I'm trying to live out my walk is through community involvement. I've jumped on the board with the Border View Family YMCA, and I recently helped out *San Diego Magazine* with a Taste of South Bay that highlighted local restaurants and businesses specifically operating in Southtown. The event was a huge success, and I know it will bring so much attention to the rich culture we have going on here in the South. I have a good feeling this will become an annual event and give Southtown the amazing exposure she deserves to all of Southern California.

What first got me connected with the event was my Youth of the Nation Foundation. *San Diego Magazine* was looking for charitable partners, and they hit me up. The long-term goal of my foundation is to create a place within walking distance of my old neighborhood that would be kind of a YMCA but geared toward music and art. A lot of teens and kids are looking for an after-school safe haven, but it seems that so many programs are athletics based. Kids whose passion is in music and the arts have no place to go.

At the Youth of the Nation facility, there would be art rooms where kids can create. There would be jam rooms with every kind of instrument, a full recording studio, and a performance hall. Everything would be new and quality. If you give a kid a busted-up guitar that goes out of tune every five minutes, they'll give up on it quick. But if you give them a place where they can pick up a quality guitar, plug it in to an amp, and crank it up to 10, they might stick around a little longer.

That's our long game. What's been keeping us busy over the last few years has been giving away instruments to schools, studios, and a local juvenile detention center. We've also provided school supplies, art supplies, clothes, and food to families who have needed it. We're trusting that when God is ready for us to move forward on the big dream, He'll let us know.

Want to hear something really crazy? To my surprise, the City and County of San Diego just recently acknowledged my philanthropic work throughout the years and officially made June 23 Sonny Sandoval Day. Can you believe it? San Diego gave this Southtown street kid his own fricking day! The best part? June 23 is my mother's birthday. Absolutely incredible. I'm beyond humbled.

MUSICALLY, I'M AS EXCITED AS EVER over what P.O.D. has going on. *Veritas* is a great album that hearkens back to our rock roots. It's easily one of the best records we've put out, and touring it will be a blast.

When I was confined to home during COVID, I was dying to find a creative outlet. I'd never had so little to do and so much free time in which to do it. So, I started connecting with no-name producers online. I'd hear a great reggae instrumental on SoundCloud or somewhere, and I'd hit them up. I was linking with guys from Germany, Argentina, Mexico—all around the globe. I'd tell them,

"Hey, man, I really dig your music. I'm just trying to put some stuff together. Mind sending me some tunes?" They'd send it off and I'd put words to it.

I love how it's turned out. It's got the feel of the early, simple days of music. They'd send me music on just a virtual handshake. I'd give it some lyrics, then put it all together here in my house. It's so easy now to do that. Just plug your microphone into your computer and go for it. I sent some of it off to the label and they dug it. But—and with labels there is always a *but*—they wanted a P.O.D. record first.

Turns out they were right. We got *Veritas* together, which is getting P.O.D. back in people's consciousness. The hold also gave me time to reconsider using the label for my reggae album. When you connect with a label, it comes with a lot of strings. Instead, I decided to hit up John Rubeli, because independent stuff is really what he's all about now. This record is a COVID home production, and it's retained that feel. I want it to stay raw. I want it to feel independent. Who knows? By the time this book comes out, you may already have it downloaded on your phone.

I WISH I COULD SAY that everything is smooth sailing now. But there are no fairy-tale endings this side of heaven. There have been numerous times I've wondered whether I should just get myself a 9 to 5 so I can have somewhat of a normal routine and financial stability. It's during those times of doubt and frustration that I have to stop and remember that God never promised an easy road. He never promised me a big house or fancy cars.

Recently, I heard this new worship song at church. It goes, "I don't know what You're doing Lord, but I know what You've done." Isn't that the truth! God doesn't have to run His plan for my life by me. When I don't get what He's doing, I just need to remind myself of His goodness toward me and all the times in my life that He has been faithful. God will never fail you, and He will never let you down. He sees you right where you're at, and He's waiting for you to trust and follow Him.

What He did promise is a worthwhile road, a road with purpose. Whatever the struggles, whatever my failures, I can still look back and say, "Because I said yes to God, look at what He's done."

Way back in my beginnings in Southtown, I felt the options were limited of where I might go and who I might become. But I was determined not to be a statistic.

God took that determination and put me where He wanted me to be. That is true to this day. Life may have given me some bumps along the way, but I'm loving and trusting where God has me now, and as always, my trajectory is on to the next adventure with Him.

ACKNOWLEDGMENTS

I've got to start by thanking my wife, Shannon, and my kids, who mean more to me than life itself. Each of you has had to sacrifice much so that I could fulfill this crazy calling God gave to me. I am incredibly blessed that God gave you to me. I LOVE you more!!

I am so grateful for the brotherhood of Ryan Ries, Brian "Head" Welch, and all my Whosoevers family. Michael Guido and Raul Ries, thank you for the spiritual wisdom and for not shrinking back from asking the hard questions when I needed to hear them. To my brothers in P.O.D., it's been a crazy ride and it's still going on. I'm just so thankful that you were the ones with whom I got to experience it all.

Huge shout-out to all my homies from Southtown. You already know who you are. Street family never dies.

A big thanks goes to Steve Yohn for coming alongside me in the writing of this book. I'm so appreciative to Zach Yoshioka of Powerline Management and to Matt Yates of Yates & Yates. To Brian Vos and the team at Baker

Publishing Group, thank you for all you've done to get this book out.

Most importantly, I am so grateful to God for calling me to this mission, leading me on this journey, never giving up on me when I screwed up, and opening door after door of opportunity to let people know through my words and my life that Jesus loves them no matter what and that He alone has the words of Life.

SONNY SANDOVAL is the lead singer and lyricist of the multi-platinum band P.O.D. (Payable on Death) and cofounder of The Whosoevers. He is a product of Southtown, the southern part of San Diego that approaches the border with Mexico. He is the founder and president of the Youth of the Nation Foundation, which reaches out to children from underprivileged neighborhoods and gives them the opportunity to find their self-worth and value. Sonny is married to his high school sweetheart, Shannon, and they have three children.

Connect with Sonny:

@SonnySandovalWhosoever

@SonnyWhosoever

@SonnyWhosoever